THROUGH THE YEAR WITH
IN SINU JESU

THROUGH THE YEAR *with* IN SINU JESU
DAILY MEDITATIONS

A BENEDICTINE MONK

Erat ergo recumbens unus ex discipulis ejus in sinu Jesu, quem diligebat Jesus.

Now there was leaning on Jesus' bosom one of his disciples, whom Jesus loved.

GOSPEL OF JOHN xiii, 23

Angelico Press

First published in the USA
by Angelico Press 2025
Copyright © Angelico Press 2025

All rights reserved:
No part of this book may be reproduced
or transmitted, in any form or by
any means, without permission

For information, address:
Angelico Press, Ltd.
169 Monitor St.
Brooklyn, NY 11222
www.angelicopress.com

ppr 979-8-89280-164-5
cloth 979-8-89280-165-2
ebook 979-8-89280-166-9

Book and cover design
by Michael Schrauzer

PUBLISHER'S NOTE

This book, hereby given into your hands, contains meditations for every day of the year taken from the spiritual diary of a certain Benedictine monk who, in the years 2007–2016, received messages from the Lord Jesus, the Mother of God, and the saints during adoration of the Blessed Sacrament. These messages, which since then have spread rapidly around the world like a mighty but gentle wave of purifying fire, were first published under the title *In Sinu Jesu: When Heart Speaks to Heart — The Journal of a Priest at Prayer*.

Initially addressed to priests in particular, these messages filled a phenomenal void in contemporary Christianity, responding with visionary clarity and depth to the crisis and call the Church faces in these turbid times. Here Jesus asks first and foremost for a rediscovery of His true presence in the Blessed Sacrament and a return to intimate relation with Him in adoration. He teaches, indeed he implores, us to understand that it is precisely this that will bring about a new Pentecost, a new outpouring of the Holy Spirit, a new spring of holiness for the Church and for the whole world.

In the text we make use of five symbols:

☧ to mark the words of the Lord Jesus

℟ to mark the words of the Mother of God

◯ to mark the words of holy people/saints

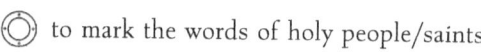 to mark the words of God the Father

 to mark the words of the Benedictine monk who wrote down these messages

May these words, heard upon the loving, beating heart of Jesus in likeness to the beloved disciple John at the Last Supper, bring forth in us the fruit Jesus most desires: healing, sanctification, and the full closeness of unification with Him in each and every day.

INTRODUCTION

☧ I speak to you to comfort and enlighten you, to show you how much I love you and want you at every moment close to My open Heart.

I speak to you because you need the assurance of My friendship and the guidance that only I can give you in this way. No word of Mine is vain. Every word that I utter is fruitful in the soul that offers no resistance to it.

The words I give you are for your instruction, for your consolation, and for the conversion of your heart in love.

The purpose of any words that I speak to you is to unite you to Me in the silence of love. That is why friends and lovers speak one to the other: to express what they hold in their hearts. Once these things have been expressed, it is enough for them to remain united one to the other in the silence that is the more perfect expression of their love.

There are times when words are useful and necessary to your human weakness and to the need you have to be reassured of My love for you, but in the end, silence is the purest expression of My love for you and of your love for Me. Little by little I will lead you into the silence of unitive love. I will teach you to imitate John, My beloved disciple, by resting your head — so full of thoughts and cares and fears and words — upon My Most Sacred Heart.

Live the message I have given you, and then make it known, for by means of it I will touch the hearts of many of My priests and bring them back to Myself. I wait for each one in the Sacrament of My love.

I desire that My words and those of My Mother should reach a great number of priestly souls to bring them comfort and courage and light. So that, through My words to you, other priests may come to know of My burning love for them and of My desire to welcome them into the embrace of My divine friendship.

THROUGH THE YEAR *with* IN SINU JESU

JANUARY 1

☧ I shall speak to you, I shall speak to your heart, so that you may hear My voice for the joy of your heart. You will hear My voice especially when you will come before My Face, when you will adore My Eucharistic Face and draw near to My open Heart. I will speak to your heart as I spoke to the heart of My beloved disciple John, the friend of My Heart, the priest of My open Heart.

I am speaking to you now because you need to hear My voice. You need to feel that I am close. It is My Heart that speaks to you. My Heart speaks to your heart so that you might live from My words, which are spirit and life.

JANUARY 2

☧ I want priests who will adore for priests who do not adore, priests who will make reparation for priests who do not make reparation for themselves or for others. I want priest adorers and reparators.

JANUARY 3

☧ When I choose a man to be My priest, I choose him at the same time to be a privileged friend of My Sacred Heart. I desire the friendship of My priests and I offer them Mine.

I have called you to experience the grace of My friendship. I want you to be for My Heart another Saint John, loving Me, seeking Me, listening to Me, abiding in My presence.

JANUARY 4

☧ Trust in the goodness of My Mother's Heart. Know that her gaze is ever upon you. Her mantle surrounds you like a protecting shield. She is attentive to every detail of your life. Nothing of what you need or suffer is insignificant to her, and this because I have given her a Heart capable of mothering My entire Mystical Body and each of its members from the greatest to the least.

Turn to My Mother in every need of yours. I have made her the Immaculate Mediatrix of all My graces. All that I would give you, I want you to have through her. Speak often of My Immaculate Mother's mediation. For you and for many souls, this doctrine is the secret of holiness.

JANUARY 5

☩ Consult the saints. Learn from them what it is to ask great things of Me, to ask boldly, confidently, and joyfully. And thank Me for the effects of My Body and Blood in your body and blood, in your soul, in your mind, in your heart of hearts.

JANUARY 6

☧ Here in the Sacrament of My love, you have everything. Here you have all of Heaven. Here you have the Creator of earth and of all that it holds, and of every human being who has ever seen the light of day. I am all yours. Be all Mine. Ask Me to unite you more and more to Myself, until you are completely hidden in the secret of My Face.

JANUARY 7

☧ To be sure, there are many ways of reaching out to My priests, and of ministering to them, but of all of these, Eucharistic adoration is the most efficacious and the most fruitful. Already My priests are experiencing the effect of your presence to Me in the Sacrament of My love. Remain faithful to this, and I will save and sanctify a great number of priests. In heaven they will be for you an eternal source of joy and of thanksgiving.

JANUARY 8

☦ This is the prayer I want you to say
in all circumstances of life:

My Jesus, only as Thou willest,
when Thou willest,
and in the way Thou willest.
To Thee be all glory and thanksgiving,
Who rulest all things mightily and sweetly,
and Who fillest the earth with Thy manifold mercies.
Amen.

JANUARY 9

☧ In the meantime, for as long as your earthly exile lasts, you have Me in the Sacrament of My love. There you have My Heart; there you can contemplate My Face; there you can hear My voice; there you can enjoy My friendship and live in My presence. I was no more really present to My Apostles than I am to you at this moment in the Sacrament of My love. Do you believe this?

JANUARY 10

☧ I loved in the face of hatred. I loved in the face of death. I loved even in the netherworld, where the just of the ages awaited My coming among them. It is by love that I vanquished hell, by love that I triumphed over death, by love that I undid what Satan, in his envy, had plotted against the creatures whom I so love and whom My Father destined for the praise of His glory.

Love is not a feeling; it is an act of the will, a movement of the heart, a glance of hope directed to My Father—for where there is love, there is confidence, and where there is confidence, the victory of love is assured.

JANUARY 11

☩ Consent to My friendship and I will espouse your soul. Thus will you be Mine in a way that exceeds every purely human notion of union, even the union between two souls in the purest charity. I created your soul for these espousals with My divinity, and your soul will have failed to attain that for which I created it, and that for which I destine you, unless you allow Me to love you and to purify you and to unite Me to yourself, not only as Friend to friend, but also as the One and Thrice Holy God to His beloved creature.

JANUARY 12

☧ Make Me the object of all your desires and you will never be disappointed. Seek Me and you will find Me. Ask for the grace of My presence in the inner sanctuary of your soul, and there hold conversation with Me, for I am in you, and you are in Me. I am your life, and apart from Me, all that this earthly life offers you is bitter and unable to satisfy your heart. I have created you and called you to live in My friendship and to long for Me on earth until that longing is satisfied in heaven.

JANUARY 13

☧ When you are before My Eucharistic Face and so close to My Heart, I am acting in you and acting upon you. Your whole being is subject to My divine influence when you present yourself before Me to adore Me.

This is why I so insist on adoration for all My priests. It is the crucible of their priestly perfection. It is the furnace of love in which I purify them like gold in the fire. It is the nuptial chamber in which I draw them to My Heart, and speak to them face-to-face, as a bridegroom to his bride, and as a man to his friend.

JANUARY 14

☩ It is My delight to hold conversation with those whom I love. Understand this: I hold conversation with you because I love you with an infinitely merciful and tender love and because I set My Heart upon you long ago to make you entirely My own.

JANUARY 15

☦ When the enemy who hates Me and who hates all whom I love saw that My love was preparing you for union with Myself, he set about corrupting you by every means at his disposal. Many things happened that put you at risk and threatened the fulfilment of My plan for you. My Mother, however, knowing of My special love for you, and loving all whom I love, interceded for you and pleaded your cause until, at last, My infinite mercy prevailed over the iniquity of the Evil One and his plans for your destruction in hell.

JANUARY 16

☧ This life of adoration is your harbour of salvation, just as it will be a harbour of salvation for many priests who risk being shipwrecked in the stormy waters of lives stirred up by sin and darkened by the shadows of evil. Thank Me that I have brought you here, and now begin to love Me more, desiring Me and choosing My love over all else. You are Mine.

JANUARY 17

☧ My Heart has a particular love for you, a love that My Father destined for you alone and for no other from all eternity. How it grieves My Heart when the unique love I offer a soul is spurned, or ignored, or regarded with indifference! I tell you this so that you may make reparation to My Heart by accepting the love I have for you and by living in My friendship. Receive My gifts, My kindnesses, My attention, My mercies for the sake of those who refuse what I so desire to give them. Do this especially for My priests, your brothers.

JANUARY 18

☧ When you have to choose between preparing a talk or homily and spending time in My Eucharistic company, choose the latter. I will give you all that you will need to say, and your eloquence will be greater and more compelling than if you had focused on preparing your words for the occasion.

Allow Me to give to you abundantly. Allow Me to speak through you, to act through you, to heal through you, and to bless through you. Trust Me to provide you with all that you need to do the things I ask of you. Fidelity to adoration is the key that will unlock for you all the treasures and infinite riches of My Heart.

JANUARY 19

☧ See how I have surrounded you with loving friends to help you remain faithful to the path of love that I have opened before you! No one of My friends corresponds to My will in isolation from others. I am forming a community of friends—of those souls nearest and dearest to My Sacred Heart—who will support each other in corresponding to My love and in fulfilling My will as I show it to them. You are one of these friends.

JANUARY 20

☧ My Heart's desire is that you should prefer nothing to your time before My Eucharistic Face, for this is the very essence of the call I have given you. Remain close to My Heart. I will not fail you nor will I forsake you in your time of need. I am attentive to you in all the details of your life and I am, at every moment, disposed to hear your prayers with kindness and with an immense self-giving love.

JANUARY 21

☧ You are but an instrument in My pierced hands. Allow Me to use you as I see fit. Above all, be faithful to the adoration I have asked of you. It is by adoration that My monastery will be built, and it is by adoration that I will cleanse and heal and sanctify My priests, the priests whom My Heart loves with an everlasting love.

Do first what I have asked you to do. Do this and I will attend to all the rest. The time is short and this work for the sanctification of My priests is urgent.

JANUARY 22

☧ I want you to consult Me in all things, even in those that seem most insignificant. I am with you at every moment in every area of your life. My eyes are upon you and My Heart is open, never again to be closed. Listen to Me when you seek My counsel, and I will speak to your heart, or reveal to you in some other way what is best for the glory of My Father and for the salvation of your soul and of the souls of the many whom I give you to influence, to encourage, and to console.

JANUARY 23

☦ I want you to tell priests of the desires of My Heart. I will give you many opportunities to do this. Make known to them these things that I have made known to you. So many of My priests have never really heard and understood the invitation to an exclusive and all-fulfilling friendship with Me. And so, they feel alone in life. They are driven to seek out in other places and in creatures unworthy of the undivided love of their consecrated hearts, the fullness of happiness and hope and peace that only I can give them. So many go forward in bitterness and disappointment. They seek to fill the emptiness within with vain pursuits, with lust, with possessions, with food and drink. They have Me, very often, near to them in the Sacrament of My love, and they leave Me there alone, day after day and night after night.

JANUARY 24

☧ Abide in Me, suffer in Me, love in Me, and I will use all that you do and suffer to repair the evil you have done and to bring healing and peace to those whom you have injured. Trust Me with your past and with its heavy burden of sin; give Me all that you have: the present moment. Offer the present to Me, and I will attend to repairing your past and to preparing your future. Your future is to be united with Me eternally in heaven by means of the same love with which you will have loved Me during these remaining years on earth.

JANUARY 25

☧ Whenever you perceive a conflict in your obligations and duties, come to Me and I will resolve it for you. Learn to depend on Me in all things. Let your first recourse be to Me, for I wait for you at every moment in the Sacrament of My love. I am never disturbed or importuned by your requests and your visits. I yearn for the company of My priests and every visit from My priests brings joy and consolation to My Eucharistic Heart. My sacred humanity is divinely sensitive to every mark of friendship and trust on the part of My priests.

JANUARY 26

☧ Do you not see how much I have been calling you to trust in Me? Trust is the key that opens all the treasures of My merciful and infinitely loving Heart. I am touched by a single act of trust in My merciful love more than by a multitude of good works. The soul who trusts in Me allows Me to work freely in her life. The soul who trusts Me, by that very fact, removes the obstacles of pride and self-determination that impede My freedom of action. There is nothing I will not do for the soul who abandons herself to Me in a simple act of trust.

JANUARY 27

☧ Will you allow Me to suffer in you, to complete in your flesh and in your heart that portion of My Passion reserved for you by My Father from all eternity?

I need your sufferings and I ask for them for the renewal of My priesthood in the Church and for the spiritual regeneration of priests weakened by sin and held in bondage to evil. By your submission to My Father's will and by your humble participation in My Passion, many priests will be healed and purified, and restored to holiness. Will you give Me your "yes"? Will you consent to this work of Mine in you and through you?

JANUARY 28

☧ My mercy has blotted out those sins that still cast a shadow over your memories of the past.

I forgive you and I heal you as I will forgive and heal those who were caught up with you in the web of evil by which the Enemy sought to destroy you and pull you after him into the abyss of darkness and torment that is the lot of those who refuse My Heart's merciful love. My Heart condemns no one to hell; My Heart grieves over every soul that withdraws from My willingness to pardon and to receive it into the embrace of My forgiving love.

JANUARY 29

☧ It is a ploy of Satan to make souls believe that I am a harsh and demanding God, that I am never satisfied with the humble offerings of My children, and that I withdraw My presence from those who seek Me, spurning their attempts to find Me, and frustrating all their desires to know Me and to know My love for them. Lies, all lies to prevent souls from approaching Me. I am, of all friends, the most gentle and the most grateful.

Come to Me, for I wait for you in the Sacrament of My love.

JANUARY 30

☧ Live the message I have given you, and then make it known, for by means of it I will touch the hearts of many of My priests and bring them back to Myself. I wait for each one in the Sacrament of My love.

I yearn to gather My priests about My tabernacles, and to draw each one of them to My Heart. I will allow each one to rest upon My breast, to listen to My divine heartbeats, and to learn of My everlasting love for him, the love by which I created him, and chose him, and united him forever to Myself as priest to Priest, and as victim to Victim.

JANUARY 31

✝ The happiness of a priest is directly proportionate to his experience of My friendship, My nearness to him in the Sacrament of My love, and My readiness to receive him there, to press him against My Heart, and to refresh his soul. The priest who allows days and weeks to pass without tarrying before My Eucharistic Face will soon find his soul drained of the supernatural happiness that is the fruit of adoration.

FEBRUARY 1

☧ Make no mistake about this: the renewal of My priesthood in the Church will proceed from a great return to the adoration of My real presence in this the Sacrament of My love. I will purify, heal, and mightily renew the priests who seek Me out in the Sacrament of My love. To them I will show My Face. I will speak to their hearts and I will make known to them the secrets of love that I hold within My Heart, and that I have reserved for them in these last days.

FEBRUARY 2

☧ In all of this, have a boundless confidence in My Immaculate Mother. Her hands are open over the Church to dispense graces in abundance, first of all to My priests, and then through My priests to souls everywhere. Call upon My Mother as Mediatrix of all graces, for you and all My priests are called to share in her mediation, as you participate sacramentally in Mine.

As for you, dear brother, beloved friend, and priest of My Heart, attach yourself firmly to My Mother by means of her Rosary, and she will never forsake you. Call upon her in every need of yours, great or small, of soul or of body, and you will understand that she is in truth your Mother of Perpetual Help.

FEBRUARY 3

☩ Eucharistic adoration is the remedy for the fear that keeps souls at a distance from Me. Why? Because it obliges one to stop, to quiet oneself with one's impulses, thoughts, desires, and projects, to abide close to Me, and to learn from Me that I am meek and humble of heart. In adoration, one who labours for Me will find rest and refreshment for his soul.

FEBRUARY 4

✝ I have charged so many of My saints to walk with you, to attend to your needs, to obtain for you the graces of repentance and illumination and union with Me that My merciful Heart so desires to give you. Some of these saints, though not all of them, are known to you. They have adopted you, some as a brother, others as a spiritual son. Their interest in all that you do and say and suffer is continuous, and they are attentive to you at every moment.

Call upon My saints. Ask for their help. Walk in their company. Invoke those whom I have made known to you. Welcome those whom I will make known to you. One day you will be united with them, in Me, in the glory of heaven where My Face will fill your soul with an ineffable joy.

FEBRUARY 5

℟ I want priests to begin to come to Knock. Knock is for all my people, but it was, from the beginning, destined to be a place of healing and of abundant graces for priests. Let this be made known to the bishops and priests of my Church. I long to be the Virgin Bride and Mother of all priests. In sacred intimacy with me they will find the holiness that my Son desires to give each of them: a radiant holiness, a holiness that will illumine the Church in these last days with the brightness of the Lamb.

FEBRUARY 6

 As for you, love Me, count yourself for nothing, and believe always that you are held safely in My paternal love for you. There are things over which you will have no control. Humble yourself before Me, adhere to all My designs, and trust in My perfect love for you. I am not a cruel tyrant. I am the most loving of fathers, the Father from whom every fatherhood on earth derives its name.

FEBRUARY 7

☧ Just as I am the perpetual Victim and interceding Priest in the Sacrament of My love, so do I intend to make you like Myself a perpetual victim and interceding priest for the sake of all My priests. Suffer and pray always. I will sustain you with My love, and the anointing of the Holy Spirit will rest upon you in such abundance that it will no longer be you who suffer and pray but I Myself who will suffer and pray in you. This is My plan for you. Tell Me that you accept it.

FEBRUARY 8

☨ The fatherhood of Love Crucified was prefigured in Abraham when, in obedience to My Father, he prepared to sacrifice his beloved Isaac. Abraham's fatherhood was broken open and, in some way, already filled the earth with descendants, when he consented to the suffering asked of him by My Father. You, too, will enter into a fatherhood wider and deeper and more far-reaching than anything you can imagine, by accepting the sufferings that I will send you, the sufferings by which I will unite Myself to you.

FEBRUARY 9

☧ Nothing surrendered to My Heart is ever lost. If you would place the persons and the things you love in the safest place of all, surrender them to My Sacred Heart.

✠ O my beloved Jesus,
I surrender to Thy Sacred Heart
all that I love.

FEBRUARY 10

☧ There are particular graces reserved for souls who keep watch before My Eucharistic Face during the night. Those who pray by night imitate My own night watches of prayer to My Father. How often would I keep vigil in the presence of My Father, conversing with Him in the silence of the night, and taking up into My prayer the secret cares of a sleeping world, and even the groans of creation. You will discover that there is a clarity and a peace in nocturnal prayer that I do not give to souls at other times.

Learn to adore Me by night. I especially desire that priests should come to Me at night. They will lose nothing of their repose, for I will be their refreshment and their rest.

FEBRUARY 11

☩ Spend less time at the computer and more time in My presence. I wait for you here. I long to see you before Me. I want to give you all the signs of My friendship that My Heart has destined for you and for no other, but for this you must come to Me. Follow the promptings of My grace.

FEBRUARY 12

☧ There are so many lesser things that pull you away, that eat up your time, and that put stumbling blocks in the path of your coming to be with Me. Learn to recognize these obstacles for what they are. Some of them are your own doing; others are the work of the Evil One; still others come from the ordinary cares of life in a world that has forgotten how to be still in My presence. Do not let yourself be stopped by any of these things. Learn to come to Me quickly, generously, and gladly. I wait for you in the Sacrament of My love, and you will not be disappointed in coming to Me. This is really all I ask of souls, and especially of My priests — that they come to Me. And I will do the rest.

FEBRUARY 13

☨ It is enough to surrender your sins to Me: in return I bestow an abundance of graces, precious graces that sanctify the soul and cause virtues to spring up where formerly there was nothing but a wasteland inhabited by the shadows of vice.

I want My priests to be the first to experience the immensity of My mercy. I want them to be the first to experience this exchange of sin for grace, of darkness for light, of sickness for health, and of sadness for joy. Let them come to Me in the Sacrament of My mercy, and then let them seek Me out daily, even hourly, in the Sacrament of My love, the Most Holy Eucharist. There I wait for them, there they will find everything their hearts desire.

FEBRUARY 14

☧ I will not abandon or forsake you. I am faithful. I have chosen you and you are Mine. Why do you doubt My love for you? Have I not given you signs of My favour? Have I not shown you that My mercy has prepared for you a future full of hope? Did I not promise you years of happiness, of holiness, and of peace? Believe that I will keep you as the apple of My eye. I hold you close to My wounded Heart. Trust that I will bring about all that I have promised you.

FEBRUARY 15

☧ It is not by privileges, special graces, or mystical experiences that souls are perfected in love; it is by a total adhesion to My will, and by a real death to all that is not My will. This life of yours will pass quickly. In the end, you will take comfort in one thing only: in the "Yes" that you will have said to My love for you, and in your adhesion to My will as it will have unfolded minute by minute, hour by hour, and day by day in your life.

FEBRUARY 16

☩ Your sufferings will be made of weakness and weariness and dependence on others. I will send you physical sufferings, but I will also strengthen your heart and unite you more and more to Myself in a joy transcending all suffering and in a strength transcending every weakness. You will be with Me on the altar of the Cross, and your life will become to the eyes of all a continuation and prolongation of My sacrifice on Calvary. Thus will you be that father in Jesus Crucified that I have chosen you to be: a father to the souls of many priests, a father with a heart pierced like My own Heart, and with an ever-flowing fountain of love for the healing of souls and the sanctification of My priests, My beloved priests. Do you accept this?

FEBRUARY 17

☧ Far too many priests become melancholy and bitter because they keep Me at a distance from their hearts. Priests think that ministry is the whole of their vocation, forgetting that I call them, first of all, *to be with Me*, to abide in My presence, and to become My intimate friends.

For many, the business of religion has driven out the joy that is an infallible sign of My presence in one's life. I Myself am no longer central to the priestly ministry of too many of My chosen ones: they exhaust themselves in a constant flow of activities and conversations, never taking time to be silent in My presence, and to listen to what My Heart longs to speak to their hearts.

FEBRUARY 18

☧ Your sleepiness in no way impedes My action in your soul. If My action depended on your state of attention, I would be limited indeed. My action in your soul is deeper than your outward states of attention or sleepiness, deeper too than your thoughts and imaginings. You have only to come before Me intending to adore Me and to offer yourself to My Heart, and I will do all the rest.

FEBRUARY 19

☧ It is not forbidden you to dream dreams or to imagine a future that you think will make you happy—I give you your imagination and I am not offended when you use it. The imagined good becomes an evil, however, when it saps you of your energy; when it drains you of the vitality that I would have you offer Me in sacrifice by being faithful to the reality that is here and now; and when you use your imagination to flee from obedience and submission to Me in the circumstances and in the places where I have placed you at this time.

FEBRUARY 20

☩ Come to Me and remain in My presence. Be My priest adorer, My reparator. Be My friend, the friend of My Eucharistic Heart, as was Saint John. He will help you to follow him in the way of a strong and tender love for Me and for My Immaculate Mother. I have given him to you, among so many other saints, as a friend, a protector, and a guide. Ask for his intercession. I am pleased that you so often refer to him in your preaching and in what you write. He is the Apostle of these last days. He holds the key to the secrets of My Sacred Heart, and these secrets he shares with those whom I have entrusted to him.

FEBRUARY 21

☦ I grieve over the carelessness with which some priests approach My Holy Mysteries. The remedy for this lack of reverence, attention, and devotion is a filial recourse to My Mother. Hers it is to prepare the heart of the priest to offer the Holy Sacrifice worthily. My Mother is full of solicitude for all her priest sons. She wants to see them go to the altar clothed in humility, in purity, in innocence of heart, and in profound adoration. She accompanies every priest in the sacred actions of his ministry. She sustains every priest by means of her all-powerful intercession.

FEBRUARY 22

☧ I have gathered into this cenacle, as into the hospital of My Sacred Heart, the broken-hearted, the empty, the fearful, and the lonely. This I will continue to do, for My Heart is the refuge and rest of all who trust in My love.

FEBRUARY 23

☧ There is a very real sense in which the prayer of adoration is a loss of one's life. It is a kind of falling into the ground to die. Remember this when you come to adore Me. Look at the Sacred Host and see Me, who am the grain of wheat fallen into the ground and risen to life, and become the food of a vast multitude of souls, and this until the end of time. The grain of wheat that I was has become the Host that I am.

When you adore Me, forgetting yourself and forsaking all things for Me, you imitate Me, for adoration is a kind of death. It is a passing out of everything that solicits the senses and a cleaving to Me alone in the bright darkness of faith.

FEBRUARY 24

☧ You have not yet understood that by coming to adore Me, you open yourself to miracles of grace and to a mighty deployment of My power in your infirmity. What I say to you, I would say to all My priests: come to Me. Abide with Me. Give Me your time, for time is the currency of friendship and the proof of your love for Me.

Come to Me, and I will make possible the very things that, in your shortsightedness, you deem impossible. To the man who values My friendship above all else, I will refuse nothing.

FEBRUARY 25

☧ Enter into the silence of the Host. Become by grace what you contemplate in faith. Here, I am hidden, silent, and forsaken by all, save a very few whom I have chosen to enter into My hiddenness, My silence, and My solitude. If you would serve Me, follow Me into My Eucharistic state. Lose all that the world counts as something and become with Me something that the world counts as nothing.

FEBRUARY 26

☩ Make the writings of My little Josefa known to the priests I will show you. They will find in them a remedy, a comfort, and a source of confidence in My merciful love. They are not for all; not all are humble enough to hear the message of My Heart, but the broken and the wounded, those devastated by sin will understand them and will rejoice in the message of My love.

FEBRUARY 27

☧ You will suffer as I suffered, that is to say, with an ineffable love. The love that will consume you and sustain you and refresh you in your sufferings is the burning Flame of Love, the Holy Spirit. My sacrifice upon the wood of the Cross was a holocaust of love consumed in the Holy Spirit. This is what I want for you, that you too should become a holocaust of love united to Me on the altar of the Cross and consumed in the fire of the Holy Spirit. Suffering is the fuel of love's holocaust.

FEBRUARY 28

℞ I desire that all priests should become aware of the infinite value and power of but a single drop of the Blood of my Son. You whom He has called to be His priest adorer and reparator, adore His precious Blood in the Sacrament of His love. His Blood mixed with water flows ceaselessly from His Eucharistic Heart, His Heart pierced by the soldier's lance to purify and vivify the whole Church, but in the first place, to purify and vivify His priests. When you come into His Eucharistic presence, be aware of His precious Blood streaming from His open Heart. Adore His Blood and apply it to your wounds and to the wounds of souls.

FEBRUARY 29

☩ I renew for you the words I uttered for Saint John from the Cross: "Behold your Mother." Live in her presence. Honour her at every occasion and in every way possible.

She desires nothing more than to look after you, just as if you were her only son. Her attention for you is not divided, nor is it in any way impaired by the attention she gives to the vast multitude of her children through the ages. Trust in her care for you.

MARCH 1

☧ Suffering and adoration are two expressions of the love that I desire to see burning in your heart. Suffer in love for Me, and adore Me out of love. It is love that gives suffering its value in My eyes and in the eyes of My Father, and it is love that makes adoration worthy of Me and pleasing to My Heart. This is your vocation: to suffer and to adore, always in love. The love that reaches Me through suffering is a source of graces for the whole Church. The adoration offered Me out of love consoles My Eucharistic Heart and wins an immense outpouring of graces for the sanctification of My beloved priests.

MARCH 2

☩ Have I not told you before that the priesthood is a relationship of intimate friendship with Me? The priests who do not understand this have no notion of what their priesthood means to Me and to My Father in heaven.

MARCH 3

☧ When you are in adoration before My Eucharistic Face, you are not idle; you are working in a way far more efficacious than any human undertaking can be. You are here in a divinely active collaboration with Me, who from the Sacrament of My love continue My priestly mediation before the Father on behalf of poor sinners.

Never doubt of the value of your hours of adoration. It is this that I have asked you to do, and I will draw from your presence in the sanctuary a great good and a superabundance of graces for My priests.

MARCH 4

☧ The things that weigh upon you most heavily, the things that cause you the most anxiety and distress, are the very things that I want you to abandon to Me. When a particular brother becomes for you a cause of worry and distress, give that brother to Me and represent him before My Eucharistic Face. You will see changes in him that only My grace can produce. When something becomes a cause of anguish, or makes you fearful, or robs your heart of peace, give that thing to Me immediately, and once you have given it to Me, think of it no more.

MARCH 5

⊕ O my beloved Jesus, show me how Thou wouldst have me spend this hour in Thy presence.

☧ I leave you free. You need not do anything. You need not say anything. All I desire is that you should be present, focused on My presence, and allowing Me to act in your soul.

MARCH 6

☧ Expose yourself often to My words. Allow them to fall into your soul and to act upon it. You will discover that the Gospel of Saint John, drawn from the Immaculate Heart of My Mother, contains within itself a power to draw souls out of darkness into light, and out of the shadow of death into the radiance of My brightness.

So few souls understand that My Gospels are spirit and life. One cannot hear My Gospel — the Gospel of My beloved disciple, in particular — without being drawn to My Heart, whence came the Sacrament of My love, by which I nourish My Church and make Myself present to her all days, even until the end of this passing world.

MARCH 7

☧ I give audience willingly to all who come into My Eucharistic presence, and like the most gracious of kings, I grant favours to those who ask them of Me. When you appeal to My Eucharistic Heart, I cannot refuse what you ask of Me. At times My Heart will give a better gift than the one for which you ask, because you ask with the shortsightedness and limitations of your mortal nature, and I give according to the wisdom and infinite benevolence of My Heart.

MARCH 8

☦ You pleased Me by praying the Chaplet of Reparation and by offering My precious Blood to My Father for the purification and sanctification of My priests. I received that prayer and brought it before My Father; abundant graces fell upon the priests of My Church in response to that simple prayer. I prefer the prayers of the humble and simple heart, prayer made without pretence, in faith, in hope, and in charity.

MARCH 9

☩ Your fatigue and your distractions in adoration are no impediment to My action in the depths of your soul.

Here, your feelings are of no importance. What matters in My sight is your humility and your willingness to endure distractions, fatigue, and even sleepiness while adoring Me from the heart of your heart. Know that even when you feel that your adoration has been a waste of time, in My plan it is something fruitful and it is very pleasing to Me. I do not see things as you see them nor do I measure their value as you measure it.

MARCH 10

☧ You, then, be silent, because I am silent; be hidden, because I am hidden; be humble, because I am humble. Efface yourself, because here I have effaced Myself in order to remain with you, in order to give you the radiance of My Face in a way that illuminates your soul without blinding you.

I withhold nothing from those who love Me and seek Me in this the Sacrament of My silent, living presence. Those who come to Me, and abide in My presence but once, if they allow Me to touch their souls...will find in Me all that is necessary for happiness in this world, even when suffering abounds and when a darkness seems to have fallen over all things.

MARCH 11

☧ Suffering, for you, is the humble acceptance of every limitation, fatigue, humiliation, disappointment, and sorrow. It is the joyful acceptance of infirmity and weakness. It is adhesion to all the manifestations of My will, especially those that you are incapable of understanding in the present moment. Suffering offered in love is precious in My sight. Accept the sufferings that I allow and that I will for you; thus will you participate in My Passion through patience and accomplish the mission that I have entrusted to you.

MARCH 12

☩ There are many ways of expressing friendship and of responding to the love of one's friend, but the one that is most satisfying to the heart is the simple act of companionship, of presence, of being together. Experience has taught you this in human relationships, but you have yet to apply it to your relationship with Me as generously as I desire. Come to Me, remain with Me. Seek Me out in the Sacrament of My love and, by remaining with Me, adore Me with tenderness and give Me your heart's friendship and affection.

MARCH 13

☧ My Eucharistic Face radiates from the tabernacle and from the monstrance into every nook and cranny of this house. This is My desire for the houses of My beloved priests as well. I want to sanctify their rectories and transform their homes into sanctuaries of adoration and of love. Encourage those priests who are considering arranging an oratory with My Eucharistic presence in their homes. I will bless them. I will draw them more intimately into the grace of My divine friendship. I will change their habits and purify the very atmosphere in which they live and work. As a result, they will grow in holiness and souls will benefit from their new-found intimacy with My Eucharistic Heart.

MARCH 14

☧ The Holy Spirit is your other Advocate, your other Friend, and I would have you live not only in His company, but held fast in His intimate embrace. Thus will you be united to Me, and through Me to My Father.

Call upon Him with humility and confidence. He will never fail you. He is, as My Church calls Him, the "Father of the Poor." He takes delight in descending upon those who are poor in spirit and He makes His tabernacle in their hearts. Seek His presence there and begin to live in constant dependence on His divine guidance. This is how My Apostles lived, and this was the life of My Virgin Mother.

MARCH 15

☧ Show yourself grateful, sincere, and interested in others and in the things that concern them, first of all in their families. Reveal to all whom I send to you My Heart and My Face.

MARCH 16

☧ Your weaknesses are not an impediment to My merciful love; on the contrary, they endear you to Me and draw down special graces upon you. So long as you trust in My abiding friendship for you, you will experience the signs of My merciful love in greater and greater abundance. I want to fill you with graces not for yourself alone, but for all My priests and, most of all, for those who have closed their hearts to Me, rejected My intimate friendship, and withdrawn into the comfortable life they have organized for themselves.

Offer them to My Eucharistic Heart. I will receive your intercession on their behalf and, through the mediation of My Immaculate Mother, grant abundant graces of conversion, healing, and holiness to My priests.

MARCH 17

☧ My love for you is unchanging. It is faithful and it is as strong as it is tender. I have chosen you to be a privileged friend of My Heart. All is forgiven; the past has been consumed in the fire of My merciful love. Trust in the love of My Heart for you. Go forward with confidence and with peace, for I am with you and you are Mine and My love will never fail you.

MARCH 18

☧ No moment spent in My presence is without value. Every moment given Me is precious in My sight and becomes fruitful for the whole Church. It is not a question of quantity, of spending long hours in My presence when the duties of one's state in life require something else. What I ask instead is the moment of pure adoration and of love offered to Me from a simple, childlike heart. Just as a mother takes as much delight in a single wildflower offered by her child as in a great bouquet of flowers, so too do I take delight in the moment offered Me out of love.

MARCH 19

☧ It is in these few precious moments after Holy Communion that My Heart seeks to hold conversation with My friends, but so many turn away from Me to busy themselves about many things. Of you, My friend, I ask something more. Remain with Me for these few moments. Listen for the sound of My voice in your heart. Know that My desire is to speak to you and to listen to all that you have to tell Me. It is in these moments that I am most disposed to grant the requests made of Me in faith.

MARCH 20

☧ Make My Eucharistic presence the very heart of your life and the centre to which you return for warmth, for healing, for comfort, and for light.

In the light of My Eucharistic Face great things take place in souls. You have only to present yourself before Me, and the light of My Countenance, veiled in the Sacrament of My love, begins at once to work in your soul. This is a secret that I would have you share with all souls, beginning with the priests whom I will send you.

MARCH 21

☧ I will teach you to imitate John, My beloved disciple, by resting your head—so full of thoughts and cares and fears and words—upon My Most Sacred Heart. There you will learn to find peace and perfect happiness in listening only to the steady eternal rhythm of My Heart, which beats with love for you and for all priests. It is not the length of these moments that matters but, rather, the intensity of divine love that fills them.

MARCH 22

☧ For one who loves, the time in My presence passes quickly, storing up immense treasures of merit for souls. The merits of your adoration I consider as belonging to the neediest and most broken of My priests.

You will not see in this life the good done to the souls of My beloved priests by your fidelity to adoration, but in heaven it will be revealed to you, and this revelation will cause you an immense increase of delight in My presence.

MARCH 23

☧ I will increase your love for Me. This is what I will do in you, because you ask it of Me, and in the souls of any others who ask it of Me, especially in the souls of My priests.

For you to love Me as I would have you love Me, you have need of My gift of love. Without Me, you can do nothing. Those who have loved Me well, My saints in heaven, glorify Me eternally for having placed in their hearts the burning love with which they loved Me on earth. Love Me, then, as I give you to love Me, and in that love you will find the one thing necessary.

MARCH 24

☧ It is in My suffering priests that I live My victimhood and bring many souls to salvation who, were it not for My Passion continued in My priests, would be lost to My love for them. I will to save souls through the sufferings of My victim priests. They are lambs for the slaughter, but I am their life, and their sufferings and death are precious in My sight.

MARCH 25

℞ I am your Mother. When I see a priest son of mine disfigured or polluted by sin, I am moved, not to judge him but to show him mercy and to employ all the means at my disposal for his full recovery from the ravages of sin. So many of those who struggle against inveterate habits of sin and pernicious vices would find themselves quickly set free from them if they would only approach me with filial confidence and allow me to do for them what my maternal and merciful Heart moves me to do.

Give me your weaknesses, your past sins, your daily faults, and I will present to my Son only the love with which, in spite of all your weaknesses, you desire to love Him.

MARCH 26

☩ Give all things to Me upon beginning them, and offer all things to Me upon completing them. Work quietly in My presence, and then return to My presence here in the Most Holy Sacrament of the Altar to find rest for your soul and to console My Heart with your friendship.

MARCH 27

☧ Always and everywhere be My priest. Thus will you carry My presence and that of My Father and our blessing, that is, the anointing of the Holy Spirit, the sweet fragrance of our charity, wheresoever you go. The priest is the sacrament of My presence. The world needs now more than ever the visible presence of My priests. The world must know that I have not abandoned My little flock, nor have I forsaken those who trust in My love.

MARCH 28

☧ This is the secret of holiness: to be led by the Holy Spirit in all things. Seek the guidance of the Holy Spirit actively. Call upon Him, for He is, at every moment, available to you. He dwells with Me and with My Father in the sanctuary of your soul. He is your Advocate against the world, the flesh, and the Evil One, the accuser. He is your Advocate with My Father.

It is the Holy Spirit who unites your soul to Mine, your heart to My Heart in such wise that when you pray, it is My own prayer that ascends to the Father as a fragrant incense.

MARCH 29

☧ Understand this, that you are My other selves. All that touches Me, all that relates to Me, all that offends Me, also pertains to you.

This is where reparation begins: in the identification of your soul with all My interests, with all My sorrows, with all that offends Me; and in the union of your soul with My burning zeal for the glory of My Father and for the holiness of all people.

MARCH 30

☧ If there are so few priests in certain places, it is above all because those that are there have forsaken Me in the Sacrament of My love and no longer live in My friendship. Let every priest present himself as a friend of Jesus, and his ministry will soon take on the efficacy and fruitfulness that characterized that of Saint John, of Saint Paul, and of My first apostles. The friend speaks with the authority that only experience can confer.

MARCH 31

☩ The Rosary has become a medicinal prayer for souls devastated by the effects of sin. It is the application of a divine remedy to all that disfigures souls created in My image and likeness. Make use of this humble prayer in struggling with the sins that cause you such distress, and you will find in it the remedy and the defence that you need and that you seek.

APRIL 1

☧ Weariness and fatigue are no obstacle to a fruitful time of adoration. They are incidental; what matters is the desire to seek My Eucharistic Face and to abide in My company.

APRIL 2

☧ I accept the renewal of your offering. It is good that you should renew the offering of yourself to Me; it is a necessity of love. The beloved offers herself again and again to her lover, and so must you offer yourself again and again to the love of My Heart, so as to live in a constant state of offering and of openness to My love for you.

APRIL 3

☨ I have communicated to your heart something of what I hold in My Eucharistic Heart: towards My Father, that in Me and with Me and through Me, you may love Him and glorify Him; and towards My priests, that all My desires for their purity, their holiness, and their fruitfulness may become the desires of your own heart and the burden you lift up in ceaseless prayer.

APRIL 4

☩ When My love is spurned, when the gift of My Body and Blood is not discerned, when it is not received worthily and adored by loving and grateful hearts, I suffer a divine affliction. That is to say, I am wounded in love, wounded in My Heart. I look to My beloved priests to console Me and to make up for the coldness, the cruel indifference, the ingratitude, and the irreverence that I suffer, hidden in the Sacrament of My love.

There is a consolation that only My priests sojourning on earth, in the valley of the shadow of death, can offer Me. Only those who live for the altar and from the altar can give Me the consoling and adoring love that delivers Me from the sorrow that constrains My Sacred Heart.

APRIL 5

☧ This is why it so grieves Me that churches are locked and that I am left for days on end alone in the tabernacle. I would draw souls to My open Heart, I would have them experience what it is to abide in the radiance of My Eucharistic Face, I would give Myself in intimate friendship to souls drawn to Me in the Sacrament of My love. I would pasture souls in My Eucharistic presence, but you, by continuing to close My churches to souls, frustrate and contradict the desires of My Eucharistic Heart. There is sorrow in heaven over this.

APRIL 6

☧ My love is a personal love. I love each soul that I have created as if that soul were the only soul in the universe, and I adapt My infinite love to the particular sensibilities and needs of that soul with all the wisdom and tenderness of My divine Heart.

APRIL 7

☧ Love Me and show your love for Me by offering Me the gift of your time. Be like the candle that exists only to burn itself out in My presence. It is enough that you are there in My presence, offering Me the flame of your love and allowing yourself to be consumed in quiet adoration.

Speak to Me freely, or simply remain in silence. I do not ask for many words; I ask for your companionship, for your presence, and for the loving attention of your heart. Thus will you attain to the union with Me that I desire for you: a fruitful union by which you will abide in Me and I in you.

APRIL 8

☧ Give Me this, the sacrifice of your time in My presence, and I will give you all else, even those things that, at the moment, seem impossible.

You may think that there are not enough hours in the day to do all that needs to be done. I promise you that every hour given exclusively to Me will be like the seed of an abundant harvest. The fruit that you will reap will surpass beyond all imagining the little you will have given Me by abiding in My presence.

APRIL 9

☩ This is the root of the evil that eats away at the priesthood from within: a lack of experiential knowledge of My friendship and love. My priests are not mere functionaries; they are My chosen ones, the friends whom I chose for myself to live in such communion of mind and heart with Me that they prolong My presence in the world. Each priest is called to love My Church with all the tender passion of a bridegroom, but to do this, he must spend time in My presence. He must experience Me personally as the Bridegroom of his soul.

APRIL 10

☩ Those who think that they can succeed by planning and by calculating and by making use of human means as the world makes use of them, these I cannot use for the upbuilding of My Church. I want the little and the poor, those who have nothing apart from an immense trust in My merciful love; I want them to come to Me and to offer themselves to My Eucharistic Heart for My own designs and purposes.

APRIL 11

☧ Nothing grieves My Heart more than the death of a priest outside of My grace. I pursue My priests — even the most sinful and hardened among them — even into the moment of death, that last opportunity to consent to My forgiving mercy, and still there are some who refuse My mercy, thus condemning Me to suffer again the grief that invaded My Heart when Judas refused to turn to Me and trust in My mercy.

APRIL 12

☧ Live each day as if you are to die. Enter each night in peace with Me and with all men. Relinquish and renounce every attachment to sin and to enmity, and every collusion with evil. Prepare to die as a victim of love offered upon the altar of My Sacred Heart. Thus will you make of your death a final priestly act of oblation.

APRIL 13

☧ Ask Me to hide you in My wounds. There is a place for you in each of My five wounds; each of them represents a refuge against the temptations that threaten you, and the traps set by the devil, who would ensnare you and rejoice to see you fall.

APRIL 14

☧ And then I will ask you to adore Me faithfully
and to make My real sacramental presence
the centre of your life, your one treasure
here below, the pearl for which you must
sell all else, and the foretaste of the glory
I have already prepared for you in heaven.

APRIL 15

☧ Until My bishops and My priests allow Me to wound them with the fiery arrows of My divine love, their own wounds — wounds of sin — will continue to fester and to spread a filthy infection of corruption and of impurity in the Church. Let each one beg Me to wound him, for in wounding My beloved priests, I will heal them, and in healing them, I will sanctify them, and in sanctifying them, I will offer glory to My Father and fill the world with the radiance of My own Face and the love of My own Heart.

APRIL 16

☧ I who am here before you, I am the Word. No book, however beautifully written, can speak to your heart as I do, for I am eternal Wisdom, infinite Love, and uncreated Beauty in dialogue with your soul. My words are not like the words of men, My words surpass even the words of My saints, though I often speak through them and continue to touch souls through their writings. My words are like arrows of fire shot into the heart and wounding it so as to inflame it and heal it with divine love.

APRIL 17

☧ I will draw you into My Eucharistic presence for the sake of those priests of Mine who flee from before My Face, for the sake of those priests of Mine who refuse the gift of My divine friendship and never linger in My Eucharistic presence. I will use you as My instrument and channel to redistribute among My priests the choicest gifts of My Eucharistic Heart. Do not be afraid. Be faithful to what I will ask of you. Seek My Eucharistic Face and abide close to My Eucharistic Heart.

APRIL 18

☧ My priests are the chosen companions and friends of My Heart. Just as I experience joy when they come before My Eucharistic Face, so too do I experience sorrow when they pass Me by or forsake Me in the Sacrament of My love. If only My priests would return to Me in the Sacrament of the Altar, if only they would give Me their hearts by beginning to offer Me the sacrifice of their time, what miracles of grace would I not work in them, and for them, and through them?

APRIL 19

☧ There is more time in a day than what is measured by hours and minutes. I am the Lord of all time, and time given in tribute to Me is of greater worth than time invested in the most wearying labours. I do not ask that you stop doing the tasks that are before you, but only that you put Me before all else, giving the best of your time and the greater portion to Me alone.

APRIL 20

 O my beloved Jesus, make known Thy presence here to those who doubt, to the ignorant, the indifferent, and the cold-hearted. Draw all—baptized and unbaptized—into the radiance of Thy Eucharistic Face, and let not a single soul escape the embrace of Thy Eucharistic friendship. Thus wilt Thou satisfy Thine own thirst for the faith and love of our souls, and thus wilt Thou satisfy Thine own Heart's longing for the love of the hearts which Thou hast created for Thyself and no other. Amen.

APRIL 21

☧ Never think that your imperfections and failures are, in any way, an impediment to the work of My merciful love in your soul. You have only to give them to Me with confidence and they are consumed in the blaze of My Heart's love for you.

APRIL 22

☧ When I instituted the Sacrament of My Body and Blood, I did so not only to unite all the members of My Body more intimately to Me who am their Head; I did it not only to feed them and to give them to drink for life everlasting; I did it also so as to remain present, close, and ever available to those who would seek My divine friendship by adoring Me truly present in the Sacrament of My love.

APRIL 23

☨ The gift you asked of Me, the gift of adoration, has already been given to you. You have only to make use of it. You will see it multiply in souls around you.

APRIL 24

☧ When I ask certain things of you, it is not to burden you, but to offer you a sure way of obtaining the support of My grace. This is why I asked you to read every Thursday chapters 13 through 17 of Saint John's Gospel. This contact with My word is a real contact with My Heart. There are many things that I give you in this way. You are not aware of them now, but at the proper time you will experience the graces that, by obedience to this request of Mine, you will have stored up.

APRIL 25

☦ Be faithful to her Rosary. It is the shield and sword of spiritual combat. It assures your victory over the powers of darkness. Why? Because it is a humble prayer, a prayer that binds the soul who prays it to the victory of My Mother over the ancient serpent.

APRIL 26

☧ I love all My priests. Even those who are sunken deep into sin and vice remain the privileged friends of My Heart, friends who have forsaken Me, their only hope, friends who have betrayed Me, friends who have broken My divine Heart with a sorrow surpassing all human sorrows. I love them all and My Heart will be their refuge and their hospice; they have only to turn to Me, trusting in My mercy and believing in My Heart's love for them.

APRIL 27

☦ Pray for priests who are dying. Pray for those who will meet a sudden death. Death for a priest of Mine is meant to be a crossing over into the sanctuary of heaven where, marked with the indelible character of My own priesthood, he will participate forever in My glorification of the Father and in My love for the Church, My Bride. Those priests who are on the point of dying in a state of sin can be saved, even *in extremis*, provided that they cast themselves, repentant and sorrowful, into the purifying mercy of My Heart.

APRIL 28

☧ I am alive in the Sacrament of My love
and, at every moment, divinely active, doing
from My place upon the altar all that
I did during My sojourn on earth. From
the Sacrament of My love I heal the sick,
I give sight to the blind, I cause the lame
to walk, the deaf to hear, and the mute
to speak. I am the healer of souls and of
bodies. Those who approach Me in faith
will not be sent away empty-handed. Those
who come to Me trusting in My Eucharistic
love will experience its healing power.

APRIL 29

☧ Too many priests have lost confidence in My mercy, and for this reason they are unable to inspire confidence in My mercy in the souls entrusted to them. One cannot speak convincingly of My divine mercy without having first experienced it.

I wait for My priests in the Sacrament of My love. Let them all approach Me to experience My mercy. Then will I make them channels and heralds of My mercy in a world that needs the divine mercy more than anything else.

APRIL 30

☧ The priest who approaches Me and who remains with Me in the Sacrament of My love is not losing his time; he is at the very source of every good thing, and I will bless his priesthood with a wonderful apostolic fruitfulness. This was the secret of so many of My saints.

MAY 1

☧ I love you, and nothing on earth can separate you from My love. I do not love you because you have done anything to deserve My love. I love you because I am all love and because Mine is a merciful love, a love drawn to those most in need of redemption.

What drew Me to you was your profound misery, your brokenness, your utter need of My redeeming and sanctifying grace. And I was drawn to you because you bear in your soul the indelible sign of My own priesthood.

When I choose a man to receive the imprint of My own priesthood in his soul, our destinies are forever linked. He is bound to Me and I to him, and this bond lasts into eternity.

I want you to live in the fullness of the graces imparted to you on the day you became My priest.

MAY 2

☧ My Mother is the shining model of every monk and nun and oblate. She is the mould in which monks are shaped and formed according to My Father's plan for each one. In order to grow up into holiness, one must enter the Virgin's heart and hide oneself, as it were, in her virginal womb. Thus is one born again into the life of perfection that I desire to see in every member of My Mystical Body. My most holy Mother is indispensable to life in Me, with Me, and through Me. One who seeks union with Me will find that union more surely, more safely, and more sweetly by going first to My Mother and by consecrating himself unreservedly and forever to her Immaculate Heart.

MAY 3

☧ When you come into My presence, pour out your heart before Me: all that you suffer, all that you question, all that you fear, give all to Me. This you do already when you pray the psalms. It was through the psalms that I poured out My own Heart to My Father, and in the prayers of David and the holy ones of Israel, My Father heard My voice and inclined to listen to the prayer of My Heart.

So does My Father now when My Bride, the Church, pours out her heart before Me in the Divine Office.

MAY 4

☧ When you offer Me your physical limitations and infirmities for the sanctification and healing of My priests, I immediately put that offering to use, and My priests experience the effect of your offering because it is an act of love, and love knows none of the limits imposed by time and space, or even by death itself.

MAY 5

☧ You needed to rest in many ways, and I provided you with an opportunity to take the rest and refreshment that you need. I am not as demanding of you as you are of yourself. I ask only that you cling to Me and prefer nothing to My love, and that you bear patiently the infirmities of body, of mind, and of spirit that I have allowed to weaken you and humble you in My sight.

MAY 6

☧ John and Mary together graced the Church by living in fidelity to the words I spoke from the Cross and by abiding in the mystery of My pierced Heart. Their own hearts — the Immaculate Heart of the Mother and the pure heart of the son — were a single channel of mercy and of light for souls. I want it to be the same for you and for all My priests in their relationship to My most holy Mother. Allow your heart to be pierced as was hers on Calvary. Thus will your heart be united to Mine through hers.

MAY 7

☧ So many souls make little or no progress in the holiness that I desire for them because they do not trust in My grace. They attempt to change themselves by making use of purely human means, and forget that I am all-powerful, all-merciful, and ready at every moment to heal and sanctify those who entrust themselves, with their weaknesses and sins, to My most loving Heart. I do not ask for perfection from those whom I have chosen to be My friends; I ask only that they give Me their imperfection and the burden of their sins, and allow Me to do for them what, of themselves, they are incapable of doing.

may 8

☩ Receive My teaching and put it into practice. I have begun to form you for the work for which I chose you and have set you apart. You will enter into the secrets of My Eucharistic Heart and help your brother priests to discover them for themselves by remaining in adoration before My Eucharistic Face.

MAY 9

☧ Adoration is the second aspect of your vocation. In adoration, and from it, as from an ever-flowing fountain, you will receive the love that makes suffering precious and makes you like Me in the hour of My Sacrifice on the altar of the Cross. The more you adore Me, the better equipped you will be to accept suffering and to live it in union with My Passion, for the renewal of My priesthood in the Church and for the redemption of the souls of priests held in bondage to the forces of evil.

MAY 10

☩ My plan for you is not the one you have created and entertained in your mind. My plan for you is the one that is unfolding day after day in all the humiliations and apparent failure to achieve great things that make up this phase of your life. Accept your weaknesses, and then offer them to Me; offer them to Me through My Mother. Place them in her hands and entrust them to her most pure Heart. Every weakness entrusted to My Mother becomes an occasion of grace and an outpouring of My merciful love into the soul that suffers it.

MAY 11

☧ Trust not in what you do for Me but, rather, in what I will do for you, for I am all love, and I am all-powerful, and you have won the love of My Heart, and I shall never take from you what is Mine to give. How have you won the love of My Heart?, you ask. By learning to say sincerely and with confidence, "O Jesus, King of Love, I put My trust in Thy merciful goodness." That little invocation expresses all that a soul needs to say to win My Heart's tenderness and favour.

MAY 12

☧ Your weakness is My gift to you. Instead of offering Me your achievements, offer Me your poverty, your weakness, your very failure to achieve great things, and I, in turn, will accept your offering and, uniting it to My own all-sufficient Passion, will make it fruitful for My priests and for all My Church. So long as you come to Me humbled by your weakness and animated by a holy desire for Me alone, I will overlook the other faults that affect you and in My mercy I will erase them and give you, in their place, graces and mercies that I have chosen and designated for you and for no other, and this from all eternity.

MAY 13

☧ I speak to souls not only by means of interior words, but also by the suggestions that come from the Holy Spirit, and by events and circumstances ordered by My most loving providence so as to allow souls to rise above the earthly considerations that hold them in bondage to the things of earth, and to be more closely united to Me, who desire the love of their whole heart, and their whole mind, and their whole strength.

MAY 14

☩ It is in silence that I speak to souls. Those who flee silence will never hear My voice.

MAY 15

☧ I will give you the gift of ministering to My priests. Even those hardened in sin will be touched by your words and their hearts will be softened by your adoration before My Face. I receive the time you give Me for them as if they themselves were offering it to Me and, in exchange, I will draw them to Myself.

MAY 16

☧ Love My Mother and all the rest will be given you besides. Love her with a boundless love, for so do I love her, and My will is that My love for her should be continued in the hearts of all My priests until the end of time.

MAY 17

☧ I love silence and I love those who follow Me into the silence of My Eucharistic presence. The Eucharist is the most silent of sacraments. Once the words of consecration are spoken, I am present, and My presence is wrapped in a profound silence. I am silent in the Sacrament of My love because there I am humble. There I lower Myself to live hidden, and often forgotten, in a silence that only the lowly of heart can understand.

MAY 18

☧ This is the immense sorrow of My Heart: that this Sacrament, which I instituted in order to remain among My own until the end of time, meets with indifference, with coldness, and with a cruel insensitivity even on the part of My chosen friends, ... My priests.... Holy Communion has become, in so many places, a routine act, a mere custom. This is why I ask for adoration of My Eucharistic Face and for reparation to My Eucharistic Heart. Adoration, especially adoration made by My priests — and by priests for priests — will hasten the change that I desire and that I will bring about in My Church.

MAY 19

☩ Be faithful to your times of adoration. Seek My Eucharistic Face, for I never cease from seeking your face. This is the mystery of My divine friendship: that I, the infinite and all-holy God, should seek the face of a sinful creature, love the sight of it, and take delight in seeing it turned toward Me.

MAY 20

 Do Thou in me and through me,
   O my beloved Jesus,
all that Thou desirest to find in me
   and do through me,
so that, in spite of my miseries,
   my weaknesses, and even my sins,
my priesthood may be a radiance of Thine,
and my face reflect the merciful love
   that ever shines on Thy Holy Face
for souls who trust in Thee and abandon
   themselves to Thy divine action.

MAY 21

☧ In how many religious houses am I sacramentally present and yet left alone with little attention paid to My abiding real presence? Make reparation for this neglect, coldness, and lack of gratitude towards the Sacrament of My love in so-called religious houses. These houses where I am neglected and treated coldly are on the verge of a great collapse. They will not stand. I can no longer bear the mistreatment to which I am subjected in such places. They have become places of business and like the worldly residences of the comfortable — and I, I am forsaken under their very roofs.

MAY 22

☧ I am here, silent and still, waiting for at least one soul to recognize My real presence and offer Me the consolation of a visit, of an expression of adoration and of love. Who knows about the friendship I offer to all from the tabernacles where I dwell hidden and, for the most part, forgotten? My Eucharistic love is unknown because so few of My priests have experienced it for themselves and because so few of them dare to make it known.

MAY 23

☧ I long to restore My priests to purity of life and to wholeness. You, then, represent them all before Me, so that through your surrender to My Eucharistic love, I may touch and heal at least some of them. Every day that you adore My Eucharistic Face and draw near to My Heart for the sake of My beloved priests, I promise to deliver and heal and sanctify some of them.

MAY 24

☧ "Without Me, you can do nothing." Why is this word of Mine so often forgotten? It is a word of immense power for the healing and liberation of souls because, understood rightly, it obliges them to run to Me in every necessity of body, mind, or spirit, and to allow Me to be their Saviour, their Physician, and their God.

MAY 25

☧ You are right to put your trust in My merciful goodness, for I am faithful to My friends and all that I promise them I can give them. I ask only that you not tire of waiting upon Me. Your human way of calculating things and of measuring time does not correspond to My own simple perception of all times and ages in an eternal now. Your prayers now will not be without effect in ages to come, and the prayer of many who prayed to Me in ages past is availing to you now. My arm is not shortened nor is My Heart closed to your requests.

MAY 26

☧ Priests of Mine — priests who serve with Me in the sanctuaries of My Church on earth, even as the angels serve with Me in the sanctuary of heaven; priests who represent Me on earth, even as I present Myself before My Father in heaven: make known the mystery of My presence! Call the faithful to My tabernacles! Tell them that I await them there, that I am no absent God, and that, even in the mystery of My Ascension, I remain bodily present, although hidden beneath the sacramental veils, to all who seek My Eucharistic Face.

MAY 27

 Mark me with an incision of fire for the work to which I have been called. Sign my soul deeply and indelibly for the adoration of the Eucharistic Face of the Son and for the consolation of His Eucharistic Heart. So burn the mark of this vocation into me that I will suffer from every betrayal of it, and from every infidelity to it. So seal me for this vocation that I will find Thee only in fulfilling it and in its perfection in the lasting adoration of heaven, where Thou livest and reignest with the Father and the Son.

MAY 28

☧ I receive your petitions and your prayers and take them into My Sacred Heart, the burning furnace of charity and the wellspring of every grace and blessing. Every prayer received into My Heart is wondrously fulfilled, for My Heart cannot remain indifferent to prayers offered in confidence, humility, and faith.

MAY 29

☧ Your most effective preparation for the preaching that I ask of you is your time in My presence. There I surround you and immerse you in My love. Any word spoken out of this immersion in My love will be supremely effective. Thus will I, through you, touch souls, and heal them, enlighten them, and set them ablaze with love for My love.

MAY 30

☩ The holiness to which I am calling you, consists in a total configuration to Me as I stand before My Father in the heavenly sanctuary, beyond the veil. Every priest of Mine is to be with Me both priest and victim in the presence of My Father. Every priest is called to stand before the altar with pierced hands and feet, with his side wounded, and with his head crowned as My head was crowned in My Passion. You need not fear this configuration to Me; it will bring you only peace of heart, joy in the presence of My Father, and that unique intimacy with Me that I have, from the night before I suffered, reserved for My priests, My chosen ones, the friends of My Heart.

MAY 31

☧ I am present in all the glory of My humanity and in all the power of My divinity; just as I am present in heaven, so am I present in the tabernacles of My Church on earth. In heaven, My glory is the bliss of all My saints; on earth, that same glory is veiled in the Most Holy Sacrament to be the bliss of My saints here below. My sacramental joy is the unfailing joy of the saints on earth. If there is, at times, so little evidence of joy among My people on earth, it is because they ignore My real presence and fail to seek Me out where I am to be found: in the Sacrament where I wait for sinners, to love them, to forgive them, to heal them, to hold conversation with them, and to nourish them even with My very self.

JUNE 1

☩ You have begun this month of June well by offering yourself as a victim to the merciful love of My Heart. I will take you into the radiance of My Eucharistic Face, and I will consume you in the fire of My Eucharistic Heart. Spend yourself in loving Me, seek My Eucharistic Face, abide close to My Eucharistic Heart, and I will do all the rest. You will lack nothing.

JUNE 2

☩ Refer all things to Me. Let nothing distract you from your essential work: to abide in My presence, loving Me for those who do not love Me; trusting Me for those who do not trust Me; thanking Me for those who do not thank Me; and offering yourself to Me for those who withhold themselves from Me — above all, for My poor priests, your brothers in this valley of tears.

JUNE 3

☩ Adhere to My will at every moment, and you will be adoring Me at every moment. I understand the complexities and circumstances of your life. Be with Me by desiring to be with Me. The desire never to leave My sacramental presence is, in effect, as precious in My sight as if you were physically before Me, adoring Me, listening to Me, speaking to Me.

JUNE 4

☧ Your poverty, your infirmity, even your inconstancy is no obstacle to My work in your soul—provided that you abandon all to Me with complete confidence in My merciful love.

JUNE 5

☩ Yes, I have called you to a life of adoration and of reparation, but I call you also to humility, to the little way of spiritual childhood, and to a boundless trust in My mercy. Adore Me, then, in the Sacrament of My love, as much as you can, and when you are unable to do this, adore Me in the meeting place with Me that is your infirmity, your weakness, and the needs of the present moment.

JUNE 6

☩ Every priest is called to be a priest adorer. Every priest is invited to experience the most fruitful hours of his ministry in the radiance of My Eucharistic Face. For every priest My Heart remains open, a refuge ready to welcome him, in the Sacrament of My love.

JUNE 7

☩ Do what you can reasonably do, and what you cannot do, give to Me as well. I am as much pleased with the offering of the one as I am with the offering of the other.

JUNE 8

☩ Live your consecration to My Mother in the practical details of your life. Allow her to form you and instruct you. You will begin to experience the peace and joy of the Holy Spirit in ways that you have never known before. Where My Mother is welcomed and allowed to do her work, the Holy Spirit is poured out in the greatest abundance, and the graces and charisms of the Holy Spirit flourish for the upbuilding of the Church.

JUNE 9

☧ It is not possible for you to remain at every moment of the day close to Me in the Sacrament of My love and before My altar, but it is possible for you to adore Me at every moment in the inner sanctuary of your soul, where I am also present, together with My Father and with the Holy Spirit.

JUNE 10

☧ Faith will not always remove suffering, but it will make it bearable, and will suffuse it with a supernatural hope. Others can make this act of faith for the ones who are suffering until, helped by their prayers, they have enough strength to make it for themselves.

You are doing this when you come before Me in the Sacrament of My love. Is this not an act of faith? Does not your adoration express utter confidence in My plan and complete adherence to My will?

JUNE 11

☩ Priests are not mere functionaries dispensing the Sacraments; they are not mere presiders over the gatherings of My people; My priests are the friends that I have chosen to be the consolation of My Eucharistic Heart down through the ages.

JUNE 12

☧ It is enough for Me that you are here. I do not ask anything else of you. It is your adoring, loving presence that My Heart wants from you. In this way, you will console Me and make reparation for so much coldness, ingratitude, and indifference. I am here for you. Be here for Me.

JUNE 13

☩ Do this for the one you have presented to Me in his sufferings. Do this, and leave all the rest to Me, following My counsels as I make them known to you, and trusting in Me to act. There is no more effective way to bring comfort to those who suffer, to obtain healing for those who are ill and deliverance for those whom the powers of darkness oppress and persecute.

JUNE 14

☧ I am always here for you, and there is no time at which you cannot come to Me with the things that weigh upon you. Come to Me and I will refresh you. I will show you the way in which you are to go forward. I will speak to you heart to heart, as a man speaks to his closest friend. Do not stay away from Me. On the contrary, come to Me frequently, as often as you can. Abide with Me. Wait upon Me. Listen to Me. And you will experience the wonders of My loving mercy in you and around you, for I am the King of Love.

JUNE 15

☧ There is no suffering that I cannot heal, and if I allow certain souls to suffer for a longer period of time, giving them no sign of My healing power, it is because out of their suffering I intend to bring a great good. You must believe this and help others to believe it, for out of this truth there will come confidence and hope, even in the darkest hours.

JUNE 16

☧ Do not be afraid. Tell Me again and again that you trust in My merciful love for you.

JUNE 17

☩ It is I who am behind all that happens to you. Nothing escapes My wisdom; nothing escapes My love; nothing escapes My omnipotence. Trust Me, and be at peace.

JUNE 18

☧ A chastened priesthood will shine with chastity in the face of a world darkened by every fleshly vice and sinful excess. A meek and humble priesthood will astonish a world obsessed with power, and influence, and exploitation of the poor. An obedient priesthood will stand in contradiction to a world that, following its master, says, "I will not serve."

JUNE 19

☩ I would have you kneel before your brother priests to wash their feet. I would have you minister to them in their weaknesses, in their brokenness, and in the shame that, too often, weighs upon their shoulders, causing them to stoop towards earthly things. I would have you speak to them words of comfort. Encourage them, bless them, assist them with the gifts that I have placed in you for their sakes. Let no priest leave you without receiving a word of consolation and a blessing. Through you I will give them a new heart and a new spirit; that is to say, I will infuse in them a desire for holiness, a new and fresh love for Me and for My Church. None of this will be your doing; I will act through you.

JUNE 20

☧ Do not dwell on apprehensions and fears of going astray. Trust in Me, and in the guidance of the Holy Ghost, who dwells within you, and rests upon you.

JUNE 21

☧ Why do My priests refuse the gifts that I would lavish upon them? Many are self-sufficient, relying on their natural abilities and talents, and thinking that these natural gifts are sufficient for the success of their ministry. But their idea of success is not Mine. And the means that they would take are not Mine. And I have no need of their natural abilities and talents. I can do more with one poor priest who, like the Curé of Ars, is humble and utterly united to Me by ceaseless prayer, than I can with a priest who astounds the world with his knowledge and presents himself brilliantly in the sight of men.

JUNE 22

☧ I will direct your prayer and fulfil the prayer I direct. This will be the effect of the Holy Spirit whom I will send upon you in a new way to be the soul of your soul, and the light and life of your spirit. Yield to every movement of My Holy Spirit and you will go forward in serenity and security, preserved from the deceits of the enemy and from the illusions of self-love.

JUNE 23

☧ When you pray for any soul, begin by uniting yourself wholly to My perfect will for that soul and by entering into all the designs of My Heart on that soul. Desire only what I desire. Will what I will. Let your prayer be a way of harnessing yourself to Me so that we might work together for souls and for My Father's glory.

JUNE 24

☧ When a priest is too familiar in ministering to souls, he takes the place that belongs to Me and to no other. He makes himself the point of attraction and steals My glory for his own satisfaction.

JUNE 25

☩ I am about to give My Mother to each priest in a new and personal way. Those who will accept this most precious gift of Mine, and take My Mother into the inmost secret of their life, will experience a marvellous apostolic fruitfulness. Where My Mother is, there too is the Holy Spirit manifested in an abundance of charisms and signs given for the sake of My Body and My Bride, the Church.

JUNE 26

☦ From the very beginning—from that night in the cenacle when I handed over the mysteries of My Body and Blood—My Face and My Heart have been present in the Most Holy Eucharist. But this is a true revelation in the sense that now, I desire to draw back the veil, and to do this I will use you. There is nothing new in what I am saying to you, but there is much that has been forgotten, cast aside, or even refused out of hardness of heart. I will use you to draw back the veil on what is, wheresoever I am sacramentally present: My Face shining with all the splendour of My divinity, and My pierced Heart, eternally open, a wellspring of healing mercy and of inexhaustible life for souls.

JUNE 27

☧ My Mother waits for souls to remember her and to return to her maternal Heart, and when they return to her, she welcomes them with an immense tenderness and joy. Never does she pronounce a word of reproach to the child who returns to her, who keeps watch at her gate, who seeks to meet her loving gaze. My Mother is the Queen of Mercy. She is the refuge of sinners. She is the safe hiding place of those who live in fear of being attacked or harmed by the powers of darkness, or wounded in spiritual combat.

JUNE 28

☧ Give Me your sins. Tell Me that you trust in My merciful love for you, and I will make you the instrument of My love for them.

JUNE 29

☩ I will leave nothing undone so that My priests may be renewed in the fire of My love. I will purify those who have fallen into the filth of habitual sin. I will heal those who are broken in spirit, and even those whose bodies are weary and limited by infirmity. They will discover that I am their Physician just as truly as I am their Friend.

JUNE 30

☧ When I find a priest who is open to My gifts, I lavish these gifts upon him. Nothing is lacking to the priest who comes before Me in his poverty, and even in his sins, provided that he give Me his poverty and entrust Me with his sins, and expose all his weaknesses to the transforming light of My Eucharistic Face.

JULY 1

☩ When you intercede for one who is ailing, it is enough for you to say to Me: "Lord, the one whom Thou lovest is sick." Leave all the rest to My most loving Heart. If you ask for a cure or healing, do so with such confidence in My love that your faith is ready to embrace My response to your prayer in whatever form it takes.

JULY 2

☧ To adore Me is to demonstrate that all your hope is in Me. To adore Me is to show Me that you count not on yourself nor on others, but on Me alone. To adore Me is to give Me the freedom to act within you and upon you, in such a way as to unite you wholly to Myself, as you have asked Me to do: My Heart to your heart, My Soul to your soul, My Body to your body, My Blood to your blood.

JULY 3

☩ You do well to love the liturgy of My Church. It is the work of the Holy Spirit who, making use of human instruments, created a prayer pleasing to My Father and worthy of My eternal priesthood. Enter humbly and wholeheartedly into the liturgy of My Church, and teach others to do the same.

JULY 4

☨ I have created you for My love, and My love alone can satisfy the desires of your heart. Enter, then, the wound in My side and, penetrating even into My Heart, drink deeply of the springs of love that will refresh and delight your soul and wash you in preparation for the wedding of your soul with Me, for I am the Bridegroom of your soul, your Saviour from all that would defile you, and your God who is love and mercy now and unto the ages of ages.

JULY 5

☧ Adore Me and trust Me to restore your energy, your health, and your joy in My service. Those who adore Me know that My presence renews the soul and the body. Experience this — as you already did today — and teach others to find in My presence the rest for which they long, the peace that the world cannot give, the joy that renews the heart, and the strength to follow Me in My sufferings, even along the way of the Cross.

JULY 6

☩ Had I given to other men the grace of adoration that I have given you, you would be tempted to allow them to do in your place what My Heart requires and expects from you alone. You must be the first adorer of this house. You will adore Me in response to My Heart's desire, and, then, from you, others will catch the spark of adoration, and so a great fire of love, of adoration, and of reparation will blaze up before My Eucharistic Face. Thus will My plan and My desire be fulfilled here.

JULY 7

☧ Do not yield to fear, to doubt, and to a purely human scrutiny of something which is of Me, and which I freely communicate to you out of love. Above all else, be grateful, and allow My peace to descend into your heart and fill you with a holy joy.

JULY 8

☩ Every priest of Mine is called to bear in his own person the mystical imprint of My wounds, for they are the glory of My eternal priesthood.

JULY 9

☧ My Heart overflows with merciful love for My priests. There is not one of them for whom I would not suffer the most bitter betrayals and humiliations of My Passion over again, so great is My desire to see every priest of Mine made whole, washed clean in My precious Blood and sanctified in the fire of the Holy Spirit. All that I suffered once — especially the sufferings of My priestly Heart — remains available until the end of time to the priests of My Church, the chosen friends of My Heart. My suffering remains for them a wellspring of healing, and from My wounds there flows for My priests a balm of purity and of love. If only My priests would approach Me and apply to themselves the merits and power of My most bitter Passion and of My most precious Blood!

JULY 10

☩ Priests must offer themselves as victims for their brother priests. This is how I intend to purify, and heal, and sanctify, and restore the beauty of holiness to My priesthood: by associating victim priests to My own Sacrifice renewed on the altar, and by taking the offering of their sufferings into My own, so as to make them co-redeemers with Myself, co-redeemers of those priests who must be brought back from the distant regions of sin where Satan has held them captive for too long.

JULY 11

☩ The Church and the world wait for holy priests. And I wait to sanctify them in the Sacrament of My love.

JULY 12

☧ You think that your inability to pray without distractions is an obstacle to My grace. Were that so, I would not have been able to sanctify a great number of those whom My Church honours as saints. Distractions, when they are not entertained wilfully, are no obstacle to My work in a soul. My grace passes through them to touch the centre of the soul wherein all is still and in readiness for My healing and sanctifying touch.

Come to Me with a lively desire to surrender to Me: that is sufficient.

JULY 13

☧ Honour My love by allowing Me to love you. There is no more effective way to grow in holiness and to acquire the virtues that will make you My instrument and the priest that I would have you be.

JULY 14

☧ I want you to live in an interior freedom born of trust in My loving mercy. I will never abandon you. I have set My Heart upon you. Love Me, and show that you love Me by giving Me all things. Nothing is too small for Me and nothing is too great.

JULY 15

☩ So much sin can be avoided and so many sins repaired by a simple act of loving presence to My Eucharistic Heart!

JULY 16

☧ As soon as something causes you anxiety or fear, give it to Me. Present all your cares to My Immaculate Mother. She is your Mother, and there is nothing that she will not do for you, to bring you to holiness and to glorify Me in the Sacrament of My love.

JULY 17

☧ Consult Me whenever you want and about anything at all. I take a lively interest in all that touches you. You are the apple of My eye.

JULY 18

☦ When you come to adore Me, allow Me to unite you to My victim priesthood. Allow Me to pray in you. Present your heart to Me as a thurible made ready for the sweet incense of My prayer to the Father.

JULY 19

☩ I would work marvels in every place on earth through the ministry of My priests if they would accept the graces that I hold in reserve for them. I would first purify and sanctify them, and then, by means of their sacred ministry, purify and sanctify a great multitude of souls, so as to make of them an offering of praise and thanksgiving to the glory of My Father.

JULY 20

☧ Adoration! Adoration! Adoration! This is what I am asking of you, because adoration is the exercise of love, and love fulfils all else. Give to no other work the importance that I am asking you to give to the work of adoration.

JULY 21

✝ Resolve to abandon yourself to My love, and then be at peace, for in this one resolution is the secret of all holiness.

JULY 22

☧ Your fidelity means deliverance from sin, healing, and holiness for a great multitude of priests. Trust these promises of Mine. I will fulfil them for I am faithful, and even the world will be obliged to see that I love My priests and that I am sanctifying them.

JULY 23

☦ Those priests who forsake all else to remain alone in My presence will be, of all priests, the most effective and fruitful workers in My vineyard.

JULY 24

☧ Do not give in to feelings of discouragement. They cause you to focus even more on yourself and on your limitations. Rather, look to Me. Seek My Face and rely on the faithful love of My Heart for you. I chose you for this work, knowing full well your history and your incapacity to persevere in the pursuit of an ideal. None of this matters to Me. What I ask of you is to trust in My merciful love. You will find the wellspring of My merciful love in My Eucharistic Heart.

JULY 25

☧ Wheresoever My priests return to prayer, there will I cause a vast harvest of priestly vocations to spring up. I will multiply My priests just as I multiplied loaves and fishes to feed the multitude in the desert.

JULY 26

☧ I came here as the King of Love to bring peace and healing to each one of you. I came to show My Heart to you and to your sons. I came to heal the long-festering wounds of childhood, and to establish souls in security and in confidence in My Heart's merciful goodness.

Receive Me as the King of Love.
Consecrate yourselves to Me.

JULY 27

☩ I ask for priestly souls to console Me and to make up for what is lacking still in a part of My priesthood. For the coldness of so many, I ask for an undivided and tender love. For the indifference of so many, I ask for a holy zeal. For the irreverence of so many, I ask for a renewed awareness of My divine majesty and of the holiness that befits My sanctuaries.

JULY 28

☧ A prayer made with sleepiness and distraction is no less pleasing to Me than one made in consolations and alertness. Your subjective dispositions do not impede the action of My grace in your soul. Learn, then, to trust in Me to do the things that you cannot do of yourself, and allow Me to work in you secretly, in a manner perceptible to the gaze of My Father, and by the operation of My Holy Spirit.

JULY 29

☩ I want you to live a fully Eucharistic life; thus will I do for you all that I desire to see in you. Thus will I deliver you from the paralysis of your inadequacies and make you a sign of My triumphant grace.

JULY 30

☧ Adore Me in My humility and I will make you humble.
Adore Me in My obedience and I will make you obedient.
Adore Me in My prayer to the Father and I will begin to pray My Father in you.
Adore Me in My merciful love for sinners and I will save sinners through you.
Adore Me in My weakness and in My poverty, and I will make you strong in My grace and rich in heavenly blessings.
Adore Me, and I will live in you.
Adore Me, and at the hour of your death I will take you to myself and show you the beauty of My Face unveiled in glory.

JULY 31

✝ I want you to go to confession weekly. This is necessary for the health of your soul and even of your body. You will experience the benefits of My merciful pardon and the saving power of My precious Blood. Prepare your confessions well. Listen to the voice of the Holy Spirit and repent of the sins that He will show you. The work to which I have called you requires a great delicacy of conscience and an uncompromising purity of heart.

AUGUST 1

☧ The work for which I have set you apart, in My infinite mercy and love for the men I have chosen, requires of you a lowliness of heart born of self-knowledge, boundless trust in My divine mercy, confidence in My divine friendship, and, in serving your brothers, a transparent purity of intention, serenity, and benignity. These virtues I will give you through your consecration to the Immaculate Heart of My Mother, the Blessed and ever-Virgin Mary.

AUGUST 2

☧ Chapels of adoration are not mere refuges for the devout. They are the radiant, pulsating centres of an intense divine activity that goes beyond the walls of the place where I am adored to penetrate homes, and schools, and hospitals; to reach even those dark and cold places wherein souls are enslaved to Satan; to penetrate hearts, heal the infirm, and call home those who have wandered far from Me.

For these reasons, the work of perpetual adoration, or even of prolonged daily adoration, is intensely apostolic and supernaturally efficacious.

AUGUST 3

☧ My presence in the Blessed Sacrament preached, and confessed, and surrounded by adoration, love, and heartfelt reparation is the single greatest remedy for the evils that afflict My Church and for the sorrows that weigh so heavily upon My priests.

AUGUST 4

☧ I have not set bishops over My flock to govern, to teach, and to sanctify out of their personal abilities and by making use of the wisdom of this passing world. I have set them as lights upon a lampstand to shine in every dark place, and I have equipped them with supernatural gifts and divine power to accomplish that for which I chose them and set them over My Church. Woe to those bishops who trust in purely human solutions to the problems that beset My Church! They will be grievously disappointed, and many souls will fall away because they have neglected to take up the supernatural weapons I have prepared for them in this time of spiritual combat.

AUGUST 5

☦ I yearn for the gift of your love in response to My love, and for your presence to My sacramental presence. How long must I beg you for your time, your love, and your companionship? I am here for you; be here for Me.

AUGUST 6

☦ The kingdom of God is present in all its fullness, though in a hidden manner, in the Most Holy Sacrament of the Altar. He who seeks out My Eucharistic presence is seeking the kingdom of God. He who approaches Me in the Sacrament of My love will find the kingdom and therein all that he desires according to My Spirit.

AUGUST 7

☧ Submit to the discernment of those whom I have set over you, and in all things prefer the mind and sentiments of the Church to your own thoughts and attractions.

AUGUST 8

☧ Speak to Me confidently and without fear of being misunderstood or judged. I know your inmost thoughts, and the questions you bring to Me in the Sacrament of My love are clearly known to Me. Nonetheless, I desire to hold conversation with you because I have chosen you to be My friend and to abide in love, close to My Heart.

AUGUST 9

☩ There is no need to be frightened or to rush into situations that have only the appearance of solutions. Wait for Me to act. Show Me that you trust in Me, and at the hour willed by My love for you, you will see My plan unfold.

AUGUST 10

☧ My priests should be the first to seek Me out in the Sacrament of Reconciliation. They should be the first to run to Me as soon as they experience the pangs of an uneasy conscience and the regret of their sinful weaknesses. Frequent confession, weekly confession is, more than ever, necessary to My priests.

AUGUST 11

☧ Adoration must become a need of your soul, just as food and drink and rest are needs of your body. Come to Me often and remain in the light of My Eucharistic Face, that I may sanctify you and do in you all that I desire to find in you. Come to Me for the sake of your brother priests who flee from My presence as soon as they have carried out their sacramental duties. I want all My priests to discover the sweetness of lingering before My Eucharistic Face. I want to draw them all to My open Heart.

AUGUST 12

☧ Be faithful, then, to the mission I have given you. To be faithful, you need only trust in Me and rely on the infinite resources of My grace.

AUGUST 13

☧ On Thursday evening you will offer the Holy Sacrifice and keep watch in adoration before My Eucharistic Face. Every Thursday you will meditate My final discourse in the Gospel of John, chapters 13 through 17. Thus will you commemorate the gifts and mysteries of the cenacle: the Sacrament of My Body and Blood, and that of Holy Orders. You will, whenever possible, share these Thursdays in the cenacle with your brothers in the clergy.

AUGUST 14

☧ On Friday, you will offer Me a suitable act of penance in reparation for your sins and for the sins of all My priests. I will look for you from My Cross. I want to find you there on Calvary with My sorrowing Mother and with John, My beloved disciple. Each Friday take into your heart, as if for the first time, the words I uttered from the Cross. Contemplate My side pierced by the soldier's lance; enter into the sanctuary of My open Heart and adore My precious Blood. Receive the outpouring of My Holy Spirit, and withdraw into silence and recollection, as did John with Mary, My Mother, when all is accomplished.

AUGUST 15

☧ Saturday is the day that, by a special title, belongs to My Mother in her solitude and hope. You will live every Saturday in her company, celebrating whenever possible her Mass and the Divine Office in her honour, and offering her a token of special filial affection.

AUGUST 16

☧ Sunday is the day of My holy and glorious resurrection. I will open your eyes to the vision of My Father and draw you with Me into His embrace. Be mindful on Sundays of the labours of your brothers in the sacred ministry. Seek for them spiritual refreshment and energy in My Eucharistic presence. Sunday evening through Monday, you will do well to recall the outpouring of the Holy Spirit.

AUGUST 17

☧ How long must I beg you for your time, your love, and your companionship? I am here for you; be here for Me. Allow Me to fill you even as you empty yourself before Me.

AUGUST 18

☧ When you ask, do so with a complete abandonment to My wisdom, My love, and My perfect will. Pray in this way, and you will begin to see wonders surpassing all that you can imagine.

AUGUST 19

☧ I have called you to be for Me another John, and this vocation of yours remains My plan for you. You have only to abide close to Me, to seek Me before all else, and to put nothing whatsoever before My love for you and the love I have placed in your heart to love Me in return.

AUGUST 20

☩ When a priest flies to My Heart and rests his head upon My breast, he is safe from all harm, and the plots of the Enemy against his soul are thwarted and brought to nought.

AUGUST 21

☩ Speak to Me freely of all the things that preoccupy you and weigh down upon your heart. Ask Me whatever questions you feel are necessary and seek My gentle guidance in all things.

If I delay in answering you, it is so that you will trust Me to reveal the answer you seek in the persons who surround you or communicate with you, in events, in circumstances, and in those barely perceptible signs of My providence by which I communicate My love to little souls.

AUGUST 22

☧ Your energy and your capacity to do other things efficiently and in due order will grow in proportion to the time you consecrate to Me alone.

AUGUST 23

☧ Adore Me always and in all places by a simple movement of your heart. Consider that wherever you are, I see you and know your heart's desire. Desire to adore Me always, and know that I accept that desire of yours with great delight.

AUGUST 24

☩ My most holy Mother accompanies you; she will provide for all your needs. She is, in all truth, your own Mother of Perpetual Help. She is your advocate and the advocate of every priest, no matter what the circumstances of his life may be.

AUGUST 25

☧ Let this become the supernatural instinct of your soul: always to come to Me, always to seek My Eucharistic Face.

AUGUST 26

☧ There are so many tabernacles on earth where I am, for all intents and purposes, like one buried, hidden, forgotten, and out of sight. My divine radiance is diminished because there are so few adorers to act as the receptors of My radiant Eucharistic love and to extend My radiance through space and into the universe of souls.

AUGUST 27

☧ The wound in My right hand is your refuge from sins of disobedience and self-will. Take refuge there when you are tempted to take the path that is easy and broad.

AUGUST 28

☩ The wound in My left hand is your refuge from sins of selfishness, from directing all things to yourself, and grasping the attention of others by seeking to take to yourself what your right hand has given Me.

AUGUST 29

☧ The wound in My right foot is your refuge from sins of inconstancy. Take refuge there when you are tempted to be inconsistent, and when you waver in your resolutions to love Me above all things, and to place Me first in your affections and in your desires.

AUGUST 30

☩ The wound in My left foot is your refuge against sins of sloth and of spiritual lethargy. Take refuge there when you are tempted to give up the struggle and to consent to despair and discouragement.

AUGUST 31

☧ Finally, the wound in My side is your refuge from every false love and every fleshly deceit promising sweetness, but giving bitterness and death instead. Take refuge in My pierced side when you are tempted to look for love in any creature.

SEPTEMBER 1

☧ You have only to prefer My company to every other companionship, the love of My Heart to the love of every other heart, and the sound of My voice in the silence of your soul to every other voice.

SEPTEMBER 2

✝ Let Me hide you as you hide Me in the tabernacle. My Heart is your tabernacle, and you are My host.

SEPTEMBER 3

☧ When I am adored in a place, My hidden action upon souls is wonderfully increased. The place where I am adored becomes a radiant centre from which love, life, and light are diffused in a world in the grip of hatred, darkness, and death.

SEPTEMBER 4

☧ Ask and you shall receive. Only ask with a trusting faith, believing that whatever I will give is best for you and most glorious for Me and for My Father. Seek and you shall find. Yes, seek, but allow Me to guide you to the object of your seeking. Seek My Face, and all the rest will be given you besides.

SEPTEMBER 5

☧ There is no need to force your prayer, as if it were something of your own doing. It is enough to remain with Me, content to be in My presence as I am content to be in yours.

SEPTEMBER 6

☧ You are still too fearful in your prayer, too attached to yourself, to your own ideas and words. Perfect love casts our fear. Be little and poor in My presence, and abandon yourself to My transforming love, to the love that radiates from My Eucharistic presence.

SEPTEMBER 7

☧ When you intercede for another, do so with a boundless confidence in My love for that soul. At the same time, relinquish every desire to see the outcome of your intercession as you would imagine or desire it to be. Allow Me to receive your prayer and to respond to it in ways corresponding to My infinite wisdom, to My love, and to My perfect will for the person you bring before My Eucharistic Face.

SEPTEMBER 8

 [WORDS OF FATHER ANTOINE CROZIER]:

Do not refuse what the Lord is asking of you. Offer yourself to Him each day, so that He may impress in the depth of your heart the marks that are the proof of His love — of that love that He wants to put in you so that you may be transformed into Him.

SEPTEMBER 9

☩ The single greatest service My priests can offer one another is the readiness to hear each other's confessions and to pronounce over each other the healing words of absolution. In this way, they carry out the example I gave you when, at the Last Supper, I washed the feet of My disciples.

SEPTEMBER 10

☧ In My presence, you are ministering to souls in every time and place. In My presence, I am using you to accomplish all that My Heart desires to communicate to souls, and, first of all, to My priests. I have not called you to build or to organize, nor have I called you to speak much, nor have I called you to appear much in the sight of men. I have called you to a life as hidden as is My life in the Sacrament of My love.

SEPTEMBER 11

[WORDS OF FR. ANTOINE CROZIER]:
The depth of the impression of the wounds of Jesus in the heart and in the soul of the priest is proportionate to his degree of abandonment to the embrace of Jesus, who desires only to unite him to Himself.

SEPTEMBER 12

☩ Love Me in this way not only for yourself, but for all your brother priests whose hearts have grown indifferent and cold. Love Me for them. Take their place before My Eucharistic Face.

When I see you before Me, I will see them, and in seeing them, I will be moved to show them pity, and many of those who are far from Me will return to My tabernacles; and many of those who have spurned My divine friendship will, in the end, surrender to the embrace of My mercy. Do your part, and I will fulfil all that I have promised.

SEPTEMBER 13

☩ Come to Me only with your problems, and allow Me to provide the solutions. When you bring Me problems, sufferings, questions, and needs, I am glorified by your confidence in My merciful love.

SEPTEMBER 14

☧ There are souls so attached to what they think I should give them in answer to their prayers, that when I give them what is best for them, and most glorious for Me and for My Father, they fail to see it.

SEPTEMBER 15

℟ Shall I tell you more of this eighth sorrow of my Heart? It is when you are lacking in generosity, when you fail to respond to love with love, when you are not generous in being present to Him who is present in the Most Holy Eucharist for love of you.

This, too, is the eighth sorrow of my Heart: that the Holy Sacrifice of the Mass is celebrated quickly, with little reverence, with no thanksgiving, and with all the attention given, not to my Son, the Lamb, but, rather, to the human presence of His minister, who, by calling attention to himself, takes from God what belongs rightly to God alone.

What more shall I tell you? Do you not grieve with me over this eighth sorrow of my Heart? Grieve with me today, and console my maternal and Immaculate Heart by adoring my Son, the blessed fruit of my womb, and by giving Him all that you are in an immolation of love.

SEPTEMBER 16

☧ Hide yourself in Me until the tempest passes by, for in Me alone is your peace, and to be near Me is your only happiness.

Trust in Me and continue to adore Me. Remain in My company and I will work things beyond your imagining.

SEPTEMBER 17

☧ Give Me your "Yes," your consent to all that My Heart holds in store for you. Say with My Immaculate Mother, "Be it done unto Me according to Thy word," and it shall be done just so.

SEPTEMBER 18

☧ I could have called you to any number of other works and to the realization of other projects for My glory and the good of souls, but this is the work that My Heart prefers for you above all others. This is the hidden life of adoration in love and of reparation that I ask of you. This is the life to which I call you. This is the life, which I am about to make possible for you in a way corresponding to My power, to My providence, and to My tender love for you and for My priests.

SEPTEMBER 19

☧ Great graces are in store for you, but to receive them you must be very little, like children who have a limitless confidence in the love of their papa. When you seek to reason out everything, to know everything ahead of time, to control everything by human means, you keep Me from acting as the God of love that I am. I ask neither for ability nor for great preparations on your part; I ask only for confidence, your confidence in Me, in the love of My open Heart for each one of you.

SEPTEMBER 20

☧ Hide yourself in Me and with Me in the bosom of My Father. Rest in Me, and be content to abide where you are not seen, or known, or praised. Do the work that I entrust to you, and then be content to disappear, once you have led souls to the contemplation of My Eucharistic Face and to the love of My Eucharistic Heart.

SEPTEMBER 21

☧ You must all be humble, little, and suspended on My word.

SEPTEMBER 22

☧ Those who would be My adorers must consent to live in My tabernacle, hidden with Me and, at the same time, loving as I love: loving the Father as I love Him, loving souls as I love them, suffering coldness, rejection, misunderstanding and abandonment with Me and for Me.

SEPTEMBER 23

☧ My way is one of gentleness, of mercy, and of compassion. I offer My Cross to souls, but I never impose it, and when a soul begins to say "Yes" to the sweet and terrible exigencies of My love, I fit My Cross to her shoulders, and then help her to carry it step by step, increasing its weight only as that soul grows in love and in the fortitude that comes from the Holy Spirit.

SEPTEMBER 24

☧ Who among My priests will survive the tribulation that is coming? Only those who will have listened to My plea for priest adorers, for priest reparators, for priests who will allow Me to befriend them, and who will give Me their time, their minds, and their hearts in the essential work of adoration.

SEPTEMBER 25

☧ You will adore Me with a great love and, in adoring Me with a great love, you will make reparation for your own sins and for the sins of all your brother priests, who, like you, fell for a moment, and still fall in the darkness of sin, far from My Eucharistic Face and far from the fire of love that ever burns for them in My Eucharistic Heart. This is your vocation and it is, in essence, simple and pure. It is to remain in love and in adoration before My Face, making reparation to Me in the Sacrament of My love.

SEPTEMBER 26

☧ Banish every doubt and hesitation. There is no time for uncertainty and fear. Go forward, trusting in My love for you and in the nearness of My Immaculate Mother, who will attend to every detail of this work.

SEPTEMBER 27

☧ Allow yourself to be moved by love towards love, and so love will descend to you and take up its dwelling within you. Where love is present, all things are possible, for where love is, there am I, together with My Father and the Holy Spirit. You are indwelt by love.

SEPTEMBER 28

☩ Be courageous, and let not the small setbacks that are inevitable in any work undertaken for My glory discourage you or cause you to call everything into question. I am with you. Do not fear.

SEPTEMBER 29

☧ Doubt is the narrow end of the wedge that separates from Me. I do not refer to a doubt of My teachings or of those of My Church, but to another doubt, one that is more fundamental: the doubt of My personal love for the soul upon whom I have set My Heart. So many begin to think, "He cannot possibly love me in this way or take a real interest in me"—and so they begin to withdraw from My friendship, to flee My presence, and to greet Me only from a distance as one would a passing acquaintance.

You must never let this happen. Know that My Heart is set upon you with an everlasting and most tender love, that I look upon you at every moment with all the delicacy of My divine friendship, and with an inexhaustible mercy.

SEPTEMBER 30

☧ Dialogue with Me, with My most holy Mother, and with My saints belongs, even in this passing world, to those whose hearts are already fixed there where true joys are to be found. For now, these joys are yours in My Eucharistic presence. The Sacrament of My love is your heaven on earth. Become the adorer that I want you to be, and you will see the heavens open within your soul; there you will enjoy conversations with Me, with My Mother, and with My saints and angels. This is the remedy for every solitude and the secret of a heavenly joy while yet on this earth.

OCTOBER 1

 St. Thérèse spoke to me thus:

 This calling that you have received, my little brother, it is love: it is love in the heart of the Church; it is the love that adores, the love that makes reparation, the love that keeps company with Love in the Sacrament of love.

Be faithful, and be courageous. You have nothing to fear. Go forward and believe in Love, for you are greatly loved and nothing will be able to wrest you from Love, which possesses you and has marked you with His seal.

OCTOBER 2

☧ There are those who find the Rosary difficult. The difficulty lies not in the Rosary but in the complexity of those who struggle to enter into its simplicity. Invite souls to the prayer of the Rosary; through it I will heal the sick of mind and body, through it I will give peace where there is conflict, through it I will make great saints out of great sinners, through it I will sanctify My priests, give joy to My consecrated ones, and raise up new vocations in abundance.

Listen, then, to My Mother's plea in so many places. Listen to her, take her plea to heart, pray her Rosary and, for you, as for her, My Father will do wondrous things.

OCTOBER 3

✝ I give you My Heart, My Eucharistic Heart, as the pledge of My fidelity and as your sure refuge in every temptation and trial. My sacred side is open to receive you. Abide in Me, and My love will triumph in you and around you for the glory of My Father.

OCTOBER 4

☧ I want you to speak to the faithful of the Holy Mass as a true sacrifice. They have forgotten this. No one thinks any more to tell them that the action of the Eucharist renews My sacrifice upon the Cross, and that I am present upon the altar as upon the Cross, as both Priest and Victim. It is the whole of My sacrifice of love that unfolds before their eyes. You must tell them this.

OCTOBER 5

 O Virgin Mary, my Mother of Perpetual Help, my hands are in thy hands, and my heart is in thy heart, and this forever.

OCTOBER 6

✝ When a priest begins to avoid looking at My Face, he has begun to alienate himself from the merciful love of My Heart. Thus will he begin, little by little, to lose confidence in My mercy, to consent to sin, and to descend into the darkness of a life from which I have been exiled.

Look upon Me for those who turn away from Me. Seek My Face for those who avoid My divine gaze. Accept My friendship for those who refuse it. Remain with Me for those who flee from My presence. This is the reparation I ask of you. Offer yourself to Me as did the little Thérèse; thus will you allow Me to love you freely, and through you, My merciful love will triumph even in the souls of hardened sinners.

OCTOBER 7

℞ As for you, dear son of mine, persevere in praying to me. Hold fast to my Rosary and beware of every ploy of the Evil One to separate you from it. My Rosary is your safeguard and your weapon in the fight against the forces of evil. At the same time, for you it is a remedy and a comfort. Do you not see how the Rosary has stabilized you? Do you not experience its healing and all its benefits? Pray my Rosary and teach others to do the same.

OCTOBER 8

☧ Act with courage, with audacity, with confidence. Act as a man, a man of God, a man configured to Christ, a man anointed by the Holy Spirit. Act also as a father, a father to the poor, a father to little ones, a father to sinners, a father, also, to the priests whom I shall send you.

Act as a physician of souls. I will show you how to bind up the wounds of the heart, even the most delicate ones, and how to care for those whom I shall send you, so that you may heal them in My Name by loving them with My Heart.

OCTOBER 9

✞ Yes, you need to be manly and resolute in carrying out My will, the will that I have shown you. The enemy will try to defeat you by insinuating imaginary fears and by playing upon your insecurities and your past sins. Send him away in the power of My Name, and step into the breach for the sake of My priests, for I am with you.

OCTOBER 10

☧ The blessing of the priest is a great means by which good is made to triumph over evil, love over hatred, and mercy over judgment. Similarly, the blessing given with the relics of My saints pleases Me much. I am glorified in My saints, and I pass through them to distribute the riches of My Heart in the universe of souls.

OCTOBER 11

☩ Any loneliness you may feel is an invitation to seek Me out in the Sacrament of My divine friendship and to console My Eucharistic Heart.

OCTOBER 12

☧ Trust Me with all things, even the most insignificant. I am like a mother to the souls who believe in My merciful love; whatsoever touches them, touches Me. If only My priests knew this from personal experience, they would be compelled then to preach it, and many souls would discover through them just how deep and all-encompassing is the tenderness of My Sacred Heart for those who trust in My merciful love.

OCTOBER 13

 Always the Blessed Virgin asks me for the prayer of the Rosary, the prayer that binds all her children to her immaculate and maternal Heart. The Blessed Virgin asks all her priest sons to take up again the Rosary, to pray it often, with attention and love. It is by the humble prayer of the Rosary that priests will be delivered from the temptations that harry them. It is by the Rosary that they will undo the machinations of the Evil One who seeks to divide, to destroy, and to bring about the downfall of those whom God has chosen for Himself.

OCTOBER 14

☧ Anything given to Me, anything placed in My priestly hands, I lift up and offer to the Father, covered with My precious Blood. It is this that makes your sufferings, even the smallest ones, precious to Me, and precious in the sight of My Father.

OCTOBER 15

☧ There is nothing in your past that I will not redeem and use for My glory and the good of souls. You will repair souls and build up My priests because I have repaired you and rebuilt your priesthood. I love you and you are Mine. Go forward with complete confidence in My protection and in My care.

OCTOBER 16

☧ Faith in this mystery of the Most Holy Eucharist grows *in proportion* to the time one gives Me in adoration. It is not enough that My priests should celebrate Holy Mass daily, even correctly and devoutly, if they do not approach Me and remain with Me, who wait for them in the Sacrament of My love. Nothing can replace the intimate experience of My Eucharistic friendship—and this is the experience that I offer to you and to all who seek My Eucharistic Face, all who offer a sacrifice of time to My Eucharistic Heart.

OCTOBER 17

☧ Your prayer of intercession for N. is pleasing to Me because it is an act of love. No act of love goes unrewarded, not in this life, nor in the next. Love calls to love. Prayer is the expression of love; it engages with divine love and so, divine love—the love of My Heart for the Father and the Father's love for Me and the flame of unifying Love that is the Holy Spirit—descends into the soul of the one who prays. Thus does your soul possess heaven within itself, for heaven is the abode of Trinitarian love.

OCTOBER 18

☧ Understand just a little the sorrow of My Eucharistic Heart that is utterly forsaken in countless tabernacles all over the world. Why do I multiply My glorious presence in so real and miraculous a way, if not to be close to the souls whom I love with a burning passion and with a consummate tenderness? And I am left alone. Often I am forgotten from one week to the next or, worse yet, I am treated like a thing, like a commodity kept in reserve in case of need. This was not My intention in instituting this Sacrament of My redeeming love.

OCTOBER 19

☧ You did the right thing in coming to Me with your feelings of aloneness. I am here for you, and you, you are here for Me, only for Me, and for no other. Do you think that I will not honour the sacrifice you made in coming to live here for Me, with Me, close to Me by day and by night?

OCTOBER 20

☧ I call My priests to learn and to practice faithfully the humble rubrics of the sacred liturgy. They are not important in themselves, but they are important in that they contain and express all the sentiments towards Me and towards My sacrifice with which I have endowed My Bride, the Church. One who dispenses himself easily from such practices is guilty of a sin of pride that opens the door of the soul to the cold and hostile winds that would extinguish the flame of faith within.

OCTOBER 21

✝ There are clouds of darkness and confusion that only the Rosary can disperse, and this because it is My Mother's favourite prayer, a prayer that originated in the heights of heaven and was carried to earth by My Archangel, a prayer echoed and amplified in the Church through the ages, a prayer loved by all My saints, a prayer of disarming power and of immense depth.

OCTOBER 22

☧ Love Me, then, and allow Me to love you with My Royal Heart. It is a great thing to be loved by the Heart of a King, and I am the King of all that is, that was, and that will be. My Heart is yours. Give Me your heart in return. Thus will our friendship be sealed in heaven and on earth.

OCTOBER 23

 O Holy Spirit, Soul of my soul, I adore Thee.
　　Enlighten me, guide
　　me, strengthen me, console me.
Establish my soul in Truth...
Today, I desire to live in Thy presence,
attentive to Thy inspirations, and
　　obedient to Thy voice.
O Holy Spirit, come into my life through Mary.
Renew and invigorate my priesthood.
Sanctify me and all priests.

OCTOBER 24

☧ Fear not. The temptations you have suffered have not separated you from the love in which I hold you fast, close to My Heart. Be on your guard, nonetheless, for the enemy of all that is true, and pure, and lovely, circles about you, seeking a point of entry into the castle of your soul. Seal every entrance and window with the sign of My Cross and with the power of My Blood, and you will remain secure under My protection.

OCTOBER 25

✝ If you had a greater trust in Me, I would teach you more and speak to you as I promised I would: heart to heart, revealing to you those mysteries that I have held in reserve for My friends, those who walk in the path traced for them by John, My beloved disciple. Learn to expect more from Me, and I will give you more. Place no limits on My merciful love for you, and you will discover that it has no limits.

OCTOBER 26

☧ Conversions that are sudden and excessive are not My habitual way of leading souls in the way of holiness. I prefer to see souls advance by little steps along a way of spiritual childhood.

Teach this little way to souls and many will benefit from your teaching. But first of all, practice it yourself by obeying My inspirations in little things, and by doing all things out of love for Me, who desire to perfect you in one thing only: love. This little way leads a soul in the path of My Eucharistic virtues, those that you see when you gaze upon My Eucharistic Face: hiddenness, littleness, stillness, silence, poverty, peace, constancy, and a radiant love that rejoices the hearts of those who come into the circle of its influence.

OCTOBER 27

☩ My Mother raises souls when they fall; she instils in them a confidence in My loving mercy, a readiness to believe in My merciful love, a desire to come into My presence and to expose to Me, the divine physician, the wounds suffered in spiritual combat. My Mother is the Mother of Holy Hope. She is the Mother of Holy Confidence. One who entrusts himself to My Mother will never fall into the pit of despair. Even when sorely tempted, there will remain in that soul enough confidence to turn to Me, and to make an act of abandonment to My merciful love that will touch My Heart and release from it a torrent of forgiveness, healing, and mercy.

OCTOBER 28

 This morning, before Lauds, the Father spoke to me for the first time:

 Faith in My fatherhood will be the path of healing for many, who, like you, were kept from growing up in freedom and joy beneath the gaze of their father. I want to banish fear from your life. I want you to feel loved and surrounded by My presence as FATHER — a presence that supports you, that will not hold you back from becoming the man that I have always wanted you to be; a presence that will allow you, in turn, to become a father, a father in My image, a father as My Jesus was fully a father in the midst of His disciples.

OCTOBER 29

☧ If they are sick in their body or in their soul, let them seek Me out, and I will heal them of the evil that afflicts them.

OCTOBER 30

☧ What I want above all else is that My priests be saints, and for this, I offer them My presence in the Eucharist. Yes, this is the great secret of priestly holiness. You must tell them this, you must repeat what I am saying to you, so that souls may be comforted by it and stimulated to seek holiness.

OCTOBER 31

☧ I am He who understands every man's loneliness, especially the loneliness of My priests. I want to share their loneliness so that they will not be alone with themselves, but alone with Me. There I shall speak to their hearts as I am speaking to you. I am ablaze to be for each one of My priests the Friend whom they seek, the Friend with whom they can share everything, the Friend to whom they can tell everything, the Friend who will weep over their sins without, for a moment, ceasing to love them.

NOVEMBER 1

☧ Come before Me with sorrow for your sins and for the sins of your brother priests and, at the same time, with an immense confidence in My love for each one of you. I call each priest to holiness, even the most indifferent and negligent among them, even the most perverted and broken. I want to heal them all. I desire that they should become saints, shining trophies of My loving mercy, worthy of being presented to My Father. There is no priest whom I have not called to holiness.

NOVEMBER 2

✝ My Mother watches over you. She is your advocate and your perpetual help. Go to her confidently with your doubts, your worries, and your fears. Trust in her maternal Heart is never misplaced, and she will never disappoint you.

NOVEMBER 3

☧ When all seems confused and inconsistent, then you must turn to Me with an even greater confidence, for I remain all wisdom, all love, all mercy, and nothing escapes My providence. Have no fear, for I remain constant even when you are inconstant. I am strong when you are but weakness. I am holiness itself when everything in you seeks compromise with sin. I am wholeness and peace when you are broken and disordered.

Come to Me, then, and receive from Me all that you, in your poverty, do not have. I will give to you freely and you will rejoice in My beneficence.

NOVEMBER 4

☩ You have not resisted My words—quite the opposite: you have received them according to your ability, and so I am making them bear fruit in your soul, and in your preaching, and in your life as it unfolds.

There is no priest to whom I would not speak in this way or in another way adapted to his hearing, provided that he believe in My divine friendship, and in My own choice, in love, of the men whom I have called to share in My priesthood.

NOVEMBER 5

☦ Seminarians are taught many things, some useful, and others less so, but are they taught to love Me, to give Me their hearts, to remain in My presence, to seek My Face, and to listen to My voice? If they are not taught these things, they will have learned nothing useful, and all their efforts will remain shallow and sterile.

Pray, then, not only for My priests, your brothers, but also for the men whom I have called to be My priests, that they may learn to *love Me* before investing their talents and their energies in a multitude of other things that are perishable and have no value except in the hands and in the mind of one wholly converted to the love of My Heart.

NOVEMBER 6

☦ The remedy for so many of the evils that have disgraced My priesthood and brought shame upon My Church lies in the consecration of priests and seminarians to the Immaculate Heart of My Mother. I saw all My priests until the end of time from the height of the Cross, and it was to each one that I said, "Behold thy Mother."

NOVEMBER 7

☩ Seek out the company of My Immaculate Mother and of the saints. Learn to live with them now so that you will live with them in eternity. Honour My Mother in the mystery of her Immaculate Conception. This is a mystery full of grace and of light for those who ponder it. It is the remedy for many of the ills that afflict My priests and poison their souls. Invoke My Mother conceived without sin and she will communicate to you something of the purity and brightness of her all-holy and immaculate Heart.

NOVEMBER 8

☧ Never let sin become a pretext for staying away from Me. Instead, let sin be a catalyst pushing you into My presence. There, in My presence, as in a furnace, sin is consumed in the fire of merciful love, souls are made clean, healed, and restored to My friendship. I reject no one who comes to Me with confidence in My merciful love. My arms are open to receive repentant sinners into the embrace of My merciful love; even more, My side was wounded, so as to give sinners a way into My inmost Heart: their hospital, their refuge, their place of healing, refreshment, and holiness, that is, separation from all that is incompatible with My love.

NOVEMBER 9

☧ Come before Me, bearing every degradation of the priestly state, every betrayal, every dark and wicked secret, and I will lift up the light of My Eucharistic Face upon you for the sake of My poor priests, sinners in need of My mercy, My healing love, and My friendship. Represent them before Me, and I will represent them before My Father.

My Mother is at your side in this work of reparation for her priest sons. Constantly she pleads on their behalf; she is the great Mediatrix who stands with uplifted hands, appealing to My pierced Heart for her sons. She has chosen you to share in this work of hers, to intercede together with her, and, in union with her Sorrowful and Immaculate Heart, to obtain abundant graces for those poor priests who are most in need of them.

NOVEMBER 10

☧ In all circumstances be humble; never insist on your own way. Present your desires and opinions simply and confidently, and then leave all things in My hands. The outcome will be according to My designs and I will not be thwarted by the resistance or shortsightedness of My human agents.

NOVEMBER 11

☩ I will be attacked in My priests; they represent My Eucharistic Face. The face of the priesthood is My Face, once again mocked and covered with mud, spittle, and blood. I will be dishonoured in the Sacrament of My Body and Blood. You will see an increase of sins against the mysteries of My Body and Blood: sacrileges, desecrations, and mockeries. This too has already begun, but it will increase until it reaches proportions that will oblige My Father to avenge the blood of His beloved innocents.

For all of this you must make reparation, serving Me in My priests and interceding for them; adoring Me in the Sacrament of My Body and Blood; and praying for an end to the persecution of the weak, the little, and the poor, those who have no one to defend them apart from Me.

NOVEMBER 12

☩ Live then in the cavern of My wounded side as in a tabernacle, and seek to enter My Heart of hearts. There the Father waits for you. There the Holy Spirit will transform you and configure you entirely to Me, Firstborn Son of the Father, His Victim and His Priest.

Why do I speak to you so often of My *open* Heart? It is because for you, My priest, it is the secret of union with Me. The wound in My side is the Holy Place of My Body, the Temple. The Holy of Holies is My Sacred Heart, and that Holy of Holies you have before you in the Sacrament of My love. Like the psalmist, yearn to abide in that secret innermost part of My Temple.

NOVEMBER 13

☧ And so I remain with you always, even until the end of time, in the Sacrament of My Body and Blood. I give *Myself* in the Most Holy Eucharist as your living bridge into the presence of the Father. This too is the work of every priest of Mine: to throw himself across the great chasm that separates sinful man from the holiness of My Father.

The representation of My Father, of His interests and His desires, is the task of My priests. One who sees My priest sees My Father because I have set apart My priests to be the images of My Holy Face in the world until the end of time. The more closely a priest is united to Me, the more vividly will he reveal My Face and, therefore, My Father, to souls.

NOVEMBER 14

☧ Believe, then, in My love for you. Go forward with courage and act with faith, trusting in the love that is Mine. There are no obstacles over which My love cannot triumph. My love is a victorious love, even when all appears sunken in defeat and bound in the fetters of death. I am the God who brings new life out of what is old, decayed, and buried. I am the God who renews all those things upon which My gaze rests. I am the God for whom nothing is impossible and whom all things obey. Trust, then, in My love for you, and go forward.

NOVEMBER 15

☧ Know that I wait for you. There is a consolation that only you can give Me. It is your friendship that My Heart desires, and this friendship of yours cannot be replaced by any other. You are Mine and I am yours. Abide in Me and I will abide in you, speaking through you, and touching souls through your words.

Allow Me to be the physician of souls and bodies through you. I want to live in you and pursue on earth all of those things that I did out of love and compassion when I walked among men in My flesh. You are My flesh now, and you are My presence in the world. It is through you that I make Myself visible to men. It is through you that I will speak to them, and comfort them, and heal them, and draw them to My Father in the Holy Spirit.

There is nothing that I will not do for souls through My priests.

NOVEMBER 16

☧ I have indeed saved you from many dangers when your priesthood and your very life were threatened with shipwreck and with complete destruction. I saved you for Myself because I love you and because I had set My Heart upon you, choosing you for Myself from the womb. My choice remains, for I am changeless, and My decrees of love cannot be undone, not even by the fickleness of sinful men. You are Mine, and I am yours, and this, forever.

NOVEMBER 17

☧ A holy priest is quite simply one who allows Me to live in him as in a supplementary humanity. In every priest I would speak and act, delivering souls from the powers of darkness and healing the sick —but most of all, I desire to offer myself in every priest and to assume every priest into My own offering to the Father. This I would do at the altar in the celebration of My Holy Sacrifice, but not only there; the life of a priest united to Me is a ceaseless oblation and he, like Me, is a *hostia perpetua*. You cannot imagine the fruitfulness of such a union, and this is the fruitfulness that I desire for My Father's glory and for the joy of My Bride, the Church.

NOVEMBER 18

☦ Life is not linear; it is made up of twists and turns, of detours and setbacks, of obstacles and of trials. It is the man who perseveres in coming to Me through all these things who comforts My wounded Heart by offering a worthy and costly love.

NOVEMBER 19

✝ When you adore Me, you give Me
the freedom to work the wonders
of My healing grace within you.

This is what I would do for all My priests, but there are very few who come to Me, seeking My Face in the Sacrament of My love, and resting close to My most loving Heart. Why do they stay away, grieving My Heart by their coldness, their indifference, and their ingratitude, when I am ready to receive them at any hour of the day or night in the very tabernacles where their own hands have placed Me?

Why are they obstinate and hard-hearted, wallowing in worldly pleasures and suffering the terrible boredom of those who look to this world and its deceits for the joy that only I can give?

NOVEMBER 20

☧ I am the keeper and the guarantor of the vocation I have given you. Events and circumstances, sickness and distractions may interfere in your response to My call, but My call remains unchanged, and I will, in My own time, so arrange things that you will come back to Me, adoring Me with all your heart and responding to My Eucharistic love with a repentant and confident love of your own.

NOVEMBER 21

☧ My priests stand in the front lines; when they fall, My Bride, the Church, is left with no defence, and he who has hated Me from the beginning will advance to cause her downfall. I will thwart his plans for the destruction of My priesthood and of My Church by raising up a cohort of adorers, priests who will adore for priests, sons of My Virgin Mother, who, like John, My beloved disciple, will stand firm in the face of persecution and remain the consolers of My Eucharistic Heart that, more and more, is abandoned and forsaken in the tabernacles where I dwell.

NOVEMBER 22

☧ Here you are safe. You are under My protection and under the protecting mantle of My most holy Mother. Let the storm rage without; as for you, remain hidden here in the secret of My Eucharistic Face. Nothing will touch you, for you are Mine, and I protect those who trust in My love for them and flee to Me in the time of trouble and disarray.

NOVEMBER 23

☧ When you are weak, come to Me. When you are burdened, come to Me. When you are fearful, come to Me. When you are assailed by doubts, come to Me. When you are lonely, come to Me. Let nothing separate you from My Heart, which is ever open to receive you. It is the Evil One who seeks to turn souls away from My Heart. It is the Evil One who sows the seeds of doubt, of fear, of sadness in souls, so as to turn them away from Me and drive them into the cold pit of darkness and despair that he himself inhabits.

NOVEMBER 24

☧ I am He who comforts you, not the one who would assault you, accuse you, condemn you, and cast you out. I am the one who welcomes you with joy. I am the father delighted to see the face of his son and to hear his voice. I am the bridegroom who longs for the sweet company of his beloved bride. I am the friend who takes delight in the conversation of the friend whom he has chosen and to whom he has bound himself by a lasting pledge of friendship. Come to Me, then, without fear, for with Me you always find a divine welcome, a loving embrace, consoling conversation, and the courage to continue in the way of life that I have traced out for you.

NOVEMBER 25

☧ The Evil One plots My betrayal, a betrayal by My chosen ones, by the priests whom I love even in their filth, their sin, and their cold-heartedness. Your role is to represent them before My Face. In doing this, you will cause many to return to Me, to repent of their connivance with the lies of the Evil One, and to return to an obedience that is loving and sustained by prayer and by the presence of My most holy Mother.

NOVEMBER 26

☧ When you doubt, or when you are assailed by temptations and fears, come to Me, and rest a while in My presence. I will restore your confidence in My plan and I will give peace to your troubled heart. Too many souls, when they are in the throes of temptation or beset by doubts and fears, avoid coming into My presence, when it is there and only there that they will find peace of heart and trust in My merciful goodness.

NOVEMBER 27

☩ The world is looking for fathers, and in My priests I have given souls the fathers whom they need. The fathers whom I send to souls are men in My own image and likeness: humble, meek, self-sacrificing, tender, and strong. It is through My priests — fathers in whom the tenderness and mercy of My own Father will be revealed to His children in this valley of tears — that the world will be healed of the sufferings inflicted upon it by the absence of true fathers. Let My priests be fathers! Let them beg Me for the grace of spiritual fatherhood, and I will give it to them in abundance.

Let My priests go to Saint Joseph. He will obtain for them this priceless gift of spiritual fatherhood, and he will guide them in the delicate and difficult work of being true fathers to souls.

NOVEMBER 28

☩ Trust Me when, for one reason or another, you take your distance from Me and no longer come to seek My Face in the Sacrament of My love, nor abide close to My Eucharistic Heart. If you do not come to Me, I will go out in search of you and bring you back to Myself, so that where I am, you also may be. Your absence is to Me a greater suffering than My absence is to you, and this because I love you more, and because My divine Heart is infinitely sensitive to the actions and choices of those upon whom I have set My love.

NOVEMBER 29

☧ This is the secret of priestly holiness. Once a priest begins to come to Me, seeking My Eucharistic Face and longing for the company of My pierced Heart, I will come to him and make My home in him, and with Me will come My Father and the Holy Spirit. Thus will his priesthood be forever consecrated and sanctified and rendered divinely fruitful.

NOVEMBER 30

✝ There is a kind of guilt that keeps souls far from Me — such guilt is the effect of a wounded pride, of a deep disappointment in one's flawed self. Never succumb to the guilt that whispers: "Stay away. It is no use. There is nothing left here for you. You are incapable of the vocation you thought you heard. Accept your failure to live it and admit that you were deceived." This is not My voice. It is rather the voice of the accuser who borrows all the voices of your past, still alive in your memory, and makes use of them to assault you with a barrage of lies that are calculated to bring you down and cause you to despair.

My voice is always one of comfort and of love, producing peace in the soul — even when My words are cutting, even when they pierce the heart like the surgeon's scalpel. Trust, then, in My words to you, and close the ear of your imagination and heart to all else.

DECEMBER 1

☧ A priest according to My own Heart will love My Mother with all his heart. A priest according to My own Heart will attend to all that My Mother desires; he will listen to her and follow her counsels.

Love My Mother, and make her loved. In this there can be no exaggeration; have no fear of loving My Mother excessively. Your love for My Mother will never approach Mine in tenderness, in filial piety, in attention to all the desires of her Heart.

DECEMBER 2

☧ There is no problem or difficulty that cannot be solved or resolved by faithful persevering recourse to My Mother's most holy Rosary. The Rosary is My Mother's gift to the poor and to the simple, to the little ones who alone are capable of hearing the Gospel in all its purity and of responding to it with a generous heart. It is to such as these — the childlike and the weak, the poor and the trusting — that the Rosary is given. It is to such as these that the Rosary belongs.

DECEMBER 3

☧ When you chant the psalms, you are giving Me all that you hold in your heart and all that makes up your life.

Let no one doubt of the singular efficacy of the Divine Office. When the Church no longer intercedes, praises, thanks My Father, and weeps over sin, an icy deathlike silence begins to spread, not the silence of adoring love, but the silence of a tomb filled with corruption.

The renewal of the Church among the nations is intrinsically related to the restoration of the public celebration of My praises: to the restoration of the Divine Office, however humbly and simply, in all those places where it has fallen into abeyance.

DECEMBER 4

 Be the image of My fatherhood. By means of the fatherly love that I shall place in your heart, be My instrument for the healing of many who did not know what it is to be loved by a father. The fatherhood of the priest is a grace that I shall renew in the Church now. It is when a priest is father that he corresponds to My designs of love upon him. The Church, the beloved spouse of My only-begotten Son, suffers in that so many priests do not know how to live the grace of their fatherhood. Souls ask for fathers, and too often they are sent away, abandoned to live like spiritual orphans.

You, be a father. Receive the graces and energies of My fatherhood in your soul. The more a priest lives his fatherly mission, the more will he resemble My Son, who said, "He who sees Me, sees the Father."

DECEMBER 5

☨ Why have so few of My beloved priests turned to Me in the present darkness and in the crisis that afflicts My Church in nearly every place? They are like the sick who refuse to see the physician. They are like the lonely who refuse to open the door to the friend who desires only to visit and comfort them. They are like the hungry who turn away from the food set before them. They are like the thirsty who will not drink of the stream that flows, fresh and clean, at their very feet.

DECEMBER 6

☩ Souls who look to My Mother as to their star shining in the night will never go astray and will never lose sight of the path that leads to Me and to the glory of My kingdom. There is no safer way of coming to Me than through My Mother and under the mantle of her protection. Those who think they can journey through this life without My Mother's companionship and intercession are blinded by a terrible pride and they sin against My dispositions made from the Cross: "Woman, behold thy son. Behold thy mother." It is My positive will that *all* souls should learn of My Mother and live in her company. It is My positive will that souls should so abandon themselves into My Mother's keeping that they will be like little children held tightly against her Immaculate Heart.

DECEMBER 7

☧ Just as no one can come to the Father except through Me, so too can no one come to Me except through her in whose virginal womb I took flesh.

If only My Mother's role and the greatness of her work, even now from her place in heaven, were better known! Then there would be a great springtime of holiness in My Church and, first of all, among My priests, for I have entrusted each one of them to her as to the most attentive and compassionate of mothers. All the resources of her Immaculate Heart, full of grace, are at the service of her motherhood of the souls of My priests.

Priests have the right and the privilege of calling upon My Mother in every need, trial, failure, and sin, confident of receiving from her help and solace, mercy and healing, comfort and peace.

DECEMBER 8

☧ The Immaculate Heart of My Mother loves all My priests. She accepts each one as her own son, and in each one she sees a friend of My Heart, a friend chosen by Me, and one in whom I want to find all the qualities of friendship that I found in Saint John. This is part of My Mother's role in the sanctification of priests. She will lead every priest who consecrates himself to her, as you did, into the deepest joys of friendship with My Sacred Heart.

DECEMBER 9

☨ This is how I would have you pray for the time being. Take the time to come before Me. Seek My Face. When you pray in this way I will draw you close to My Heart. Pray using My Mother's Rosary, even when you feel that your prayer is empty or mechanical, or when you are beset by distractions. The decision to pray pleases My Sacred Heart and the Immaculate Heart of My Mother.

DECEMBER 10

℟ I am pleased that you want to imitate my son Saint John in making your home with me, in opening to me every part of your life. In this way, you allow me to act upon you, but you also allow me to act with you and through you. My presence and my action are revealed in gentleness, in sweetness, and in mercy. I want you to resemble me spiritually, just as my Jesus resembled me physically. Jesus, looking at me, saw the perfect reflection of all the dispositions and virtues of His adorable Heart. I, looking at you, want to see my own Immaculate Heart mirrored in yours. I want to communicate to you and to all my priest sons the virtues of my Heart. By consecrating yourself to me, you have made this possible.

DECEMBER 11

℞ I am not distant. I hear every prayer addressed to me. My maternal Heart is moved to pity when my children, and especially my priest sons, have recourse to me in their needs. I am the Mother of Mercy, MATER MISERICORDIAE, honoured by the Church in her chant to me. I do turn towards you my eyes of mercy, and I am ever willing to help poor sinners. Let sinners come to me; I will never turn them away. Let them appeal to my Sorrowful and Immaculate Heart; they will never be disappointed.

DECEMBER 12

☩ I never wanted to leave you alone on earth; this is why I have always surrounded you with My saints. I wanted, and want still, that you should find in them a true friendship, a friendship that is all pure, a friendship that does not disappoint. Through the saints and by their ceaseless intercession for you before My Face, you will, at length, come to Me in glory. Do not cease invoking My saints and teach others to seek from them the help they need in the trials of this life on earth. In heaven, the saints will all be glad for having helped you make your way to Me in glory.

DECEMBER 13

☧ I am your Friend, and I have chosen you to be the friend of My Eucharistic Heart. Why then would I not listen to your prayers and, in My infinite wisdom and merciful love, respond to them as I see fit?

Trust that My response to your prayers is always the best of all possible responses, and never fail to thank Me, even as you make your petitions, for no prayer of yours goes unanswered.

DECEMBER 14

✝ With Me, in My presence, is all that your heart desires. Do not look outside of Me for anything to fulfil your heart's desires. Instead, hide yourself in Me, as I hide myself for love of you in the Most Holy Sacrament of the Altar.

DECEMBER 15

☧ John made reparation for Peter's denial of Me, not by standing in judgment over Peter, whom he honoured and loved as a father, but by weeping with Peter, and by offering himself in reparation for Peter's fall.

Again, it was John who offered Me faithful love in exchange for Judas's faithless betrayal. He made reparation to My Heart that suffered so grievously when Judas walked out of the cenacle into the night. In that moment, John gave Me all the love of his heart, begging Me to accept it in reparation for Judas's cold and calculated plot against Me.

Be another Saint John for My Heart. Offer Me reparation by offering Me *yourself*: in the place of those who flee from before My Eucharistic Face; in the place of those who cannot bear to remain in My presence, close to My Heart; in the place of those priests of Mine who have time for all else, except for Me.

DECEMBER 16

☧ You experience distractions at Holy Mass and during your prayer because you have not yet allowed My order to reign over your heart and in your life. This is My desire: that your whole life should reflect, even now, the order and beauty that characterize My kingdom.

This is also My Mother's desire for you, and she will help you to attain it. Listen for her guidance and her inspirations and follow her wise direction. In this, she is the pure instrument of the Holy Spirit, who at every moment brings order out of chaos, peace out of dissension, and unity out of multiplicity. Allow My Mother to re-order your life, and you will discover the joy of living in a holy simplicity, in an order that anticipates the glorious order prepared for all My saints in heaven.

DECEMBER 17

☧ No soul need ever be afraid of meeting My gaze, for in My eyes there is naught but mercy and love.

Those who turn away from My gaze, those who fear the encounter with Me face-to-face, are those who fall away from My love.

Whenever a soul seeks My gaze, My Heart is moved to show that soul an immense pity, to lift her out of the sin into which she has fallen, to bind up her wounds, and restore her to the joys of friendship with My Heart.

DECEMBER 18

☧ Who will speak to souls of My Mother? Who will tell them that they need not fear the darkness of the night, so long as My Mother is near? Who will tell them that souls entrusted to My Mother are protected, and guided, and led along the path that I have laid out for each one? There is no better way of fulfilling one's mission in this life than by giving oneself over to My Mother in an act of irrevocable and total consecration.

Those who have made such an act know of what I speak. My Mother honours every consecration made to her Sorrowful and Immaculate Heart, and even if one should forget that one has uttered such a prayer, My Mother does not forget it. She remains faithful to her own children, even when these are distracted by the world and turn away from her brightness shining like a star over the stormy seas of life.

DECEMBER 19

☧ I desire your company. I long for the attention of your heart and for the consolation of your adoration, your reparation, and your love.

DECEMBER 20

☧ The practice of adoration is not difficult. It is a gentle abiding in My presence, a resting in the radiance of My Eucharistic Face, a closeness to My Eucharistic Heart. Words, though sometimes helpful, are not necessary, nor are thoughts. What I seek from one who would adore Me in spirit and in truth is a heart aflame with love, a heart content to abide in My presence, silent and still, engaged only in the act of loving Me and of receiving My love. Though this is not difficult, it is, all the same, My own gift to the soul who asks for it. Ask, then, for the gift of adoration.

DECEMBER 21

☦ One who makes reparation for My priests
will discover on the last day that his
own sins, though they be many, will be
covered over by a single act of reparation,
for reparation is the exercise of love,
and love covers a multitude of sins.

Love Me, and you will fulfil all that
I am asking of you. Love Me, and
I will fulfil all that you ask of Me.

DECEMBER 22

☩ This is what I desire for My priests, not a holiness that is excessive in its demands and harsh in its exigencies, but one that is entirely childlike, peaceful, and humble. This is the imitation of My Eucharistic life, and it is this that I want for you and from you.

DECEMBER 23

☩ The "Yes" of even one soul to My merciful love is of immense benefit to a multitude of souls who fear to say it, or who are hardened in the refusal of My love.

DECEMBER 24

☧ Believe in My love for you. I will never abandon you, never disappoint you. My plans are for your happiness, for your holiness, for your peace. Have no fear. I will do for you all that I have promised, and your heart will rejoice, and you will praise and glorify Me forever.

DECEMBER 25

☩ The angels are like living flames who burn in My Eucharistic presence, without ever being consumed. Yet for all of this, My angels cannot replace a single human heart in My presence. What I look for from men, what I wait for, above all, from My priests, My angels cannot give Me.

DECEMBER 26

☧ Love My hiddenness and hide yourself in Me. Withdraw from all that solicits your attention, your energy, and your time into the secret of My Eucharistic Face.

Apart from those souls whom I call to this life of adoration, such a hiddenness will appear foolish and inhuman, but it will act as a leaven upon the whole mass of dough until it rises and becomes a perfect loaf fit for My oblation. It is a spark of light being kept burning for a world plunged into darkness. It is a drop of divine sweetness in a sea of bitterness and misery. It is a presence of love in a world from which love is absent.

DECEMBER 27

☧ I remain unknown. I am left alone. Even those who claim to profess the mystery of My real presence in the Sacrament of the Altar forsake Me. I am treated with a terrible indifference, with coldness, and with a lack of respect that causes the angels to weep because they cannot offer Me reparation for the coldness and indifference of human hearts. Only men can make reparation for men. What is lacking is the loving response of a human heart to My Eucharistic Heart, pierced, alive, and beating in the Sacrament of the Altar. Only a human heart can make reparation for a human heart. For this reason the angels are sorrowful.

DECEMBER 28

 I abandon into the most pure hands of Thy Mother,
  my Mother,
all that I am, all that I have been, and all that Thou,
in the boundless mercy of Thy Eucharistic Heart,
wouldst have me be for Thee, O my beloved Jesus,
for Thy Mystical Body, Thy Bride, the Church,
and for the glory of Thy Father. Amen.

DECEMBER 29

☩ I have chosen you to be for Me another John, a friend for My Heart, a consoler in My loneliness, an advocate on behalf of poor sinners, especially on behalf of fallen priests and those who have lost hope in My infinite mercy. Be a companion for Me in the Sacrament of My love, the Sacrament of My divine companionship for every human wayfarer in this valley of tears.

DECEMBER 30

☧ There is a special grace that I have attached to the Office of Matins for those who, by vocation, are called to it. Recite it quietly and peacefully in My presence, and I will visit your soul with the sweetness of My divine love and with the fragrance of My presence within you. I am consoled when souls rise while it is still dark, and make their way to My tabernacle to chant My praises and to unite themselves to My own adoration of the Father. The psalms will unite you to My Heart, and you will emerge from the Night Office refreshed and strengthened in love.

DECEMBER 31

☧ I live in the Sacrament of My love as I live in heaven, in a ceaseless state of intercession for all who believe in Me and come to Me with the weight of life's burdens and sorrows. There is nothing that I will not do for the soul who approaches Me with confidence.

For this reason did I wish to remain present in the Sacrament of My love until the end of time: so that souls might know where to find Me, and approach Me easily, certain of being heard, and trusting in the mercy of My Heart for a world marked by suffering and ravaged by sin. There is no form of intercessory prayer more efficacious than that of the soul who approaches My Eucharistic presence, certain of finding Me and certain of being heard. I am not distant from souls in need. I have made Myself close to them, as close as the nearest tabernacle.

THE CHAPLET OF REPARATION

Or, Offering of the Precious Blood for Priests

This chaplet of reparation and intercession is meant to be prayed on an ordinary five decade rosary.

Incline (✠) unto my aid, O God; O
  Lord, make haste to help me.
Glory be to the Father, and to the
  Son, and to the Holy Spirit;
As it was in the beginning, is now, and ever
  shall be, world without end. Amen.
Alleluia. (*After Septuagesima*: Praise be to Thee,
  O Lord, King of eternal glory.)

On the Our Father beads:

Eternal Father, I offer Thee
the Precious Blood of Thy Beloved Son,
our Lord Jesus Christ,
the Lamb without blemish or spot,
in reparation for my sins
and for the sins of all Thy priests.

On the Hail Mary beads:

By Thy Precious Blood, O Jesus,
    purify and sanctify Thy priests.

In place of the Glory be to the Father:

O Father, from whom all fatherhood in
    heaven and on earth is named,
have mercy on all Thy priests, and wash
    them in the Blood of the Lamb.

LIST OF SOURCES

INTRODUCTION
In Sinu Jesu, November 29, 2008
In Sinu Jesu, November 6, 2011
In Sinu Jesu, September 23, 2011
In Sinu Jesu, March 21, 2009
In Sinu Jesu, January 30, 2012
In Sinu Jesu, January 18, 2010

JANUARY
January 1: *In Sinu Jesu*, October 8, 2007
January 2: *In Sinu Jesu*, October 3, 2007
January 3: *In Sinu Jesu*, January 3, 2008
January 4: *In Sinu Jesu*, January 3, 2008
January 5: *In Sinu Jesu*, January 3, 2008
January 6: *In Sinu Jesu*, January 2, 2010
January 7: *In Sinu Jesu*, January 7, 2010
January 8: *In Sinu Jesu*, January 8, 2010
January 9: *In Sinu Jesu*, January 9, 2010
January 10: *In Sinu Jesu*, January 10, 2010
January 11: *In Sinu Jesu*, January 9, 2010
January 12: *In Sinu Jesu*, January 9, 2010
January 13: *In Sinu Jesu*, January 9, 2010
January 14: *In Sinu Jesu*, January 9, 2010
January 15: *In Sinu Jesu*, January 9, 2010
January 16: *In Sinu Jesu*, January 9, 2010
January 17: *In Sinu Jesu*, January 17, 2008
January 18: *In Sinu Jesu*, January 18, 2010
January 19: *In Sinu Jesu*, January 19, 2010

January 20: *In Sinu Jesu*, January 19, 2010
January 21: *In Sinu Jesu*, January 19, 2010
January 22: *In Sinu Jesu*, January 22, 2010
January 23: *In Sinu Jesu*, January 17, 2008
January 24: *In Sinu Jesu*, January 24, 2010
January 25: *In Sinu Jesu*, January 19, 2010
January 26: *In Sinu Jesu*, January 26, 2010
January 27: *In Sinu Jesu*, January 27, 2010
January 28: *In Sinu Jesu*, January 28, 2010
January 29: *In Sinu Jesu*, January 28, 2012
January 30: *In Sinu Jesu*, January 30, 2012
January 31: *In Sinu Jesu*, January 31, 2012

FEBRUARY

February 1: *In Sinu Jesu*, February 1, 2008
February 2: *In Sinu Jesu*, February 1, 2008
February 3: *In Sinu Jesu*, February 3, 2012
February 4: *In Sinu Jesu*, January 30, 2010
February 5: *In Sinu Jesu*, February 5, 2008
February 6: *In Sinu Jesu*, February 6, 2012
February 7: *In Sinu Jesu*, February 7, 2010
February 8: *In Sinu Jesu*, February 8, 2010
February 9: *In Sinu Jesu*, February 9, 2010
February 10: *In Sinu Jesu*, February 10, 2008
February 11: *In Sinu Jesu*, February 11, 2009
February 12: *In Sinu Jesu*, February 12, 2009
February 13: *In Sinu Jesu*, February 13, 2009
February 14: *In Sinu Jesu*, February 14, 2008
February 15: *In Sinu Jesu*, February 19, 2011

February 16: *In Sinu Jesu*, January 27, 2010
February 17: *In Sinu Jesu*, January 31, 2012
February 18: *In Sinu Jesu*, February 14, 2010
February 19: *In Sinu Jesu*, February 19, 2011
February 20: *In Sinu Jesu*, February 14, 2008
February 21: *In Sinu Jesu*, February 21, 2008
February 22: *In Sinu Jesu*, February 22, 2012
February 23: *In Sinu Jesu*, February 25, 2016
February 24: *In Sinu Jesu*, February 4, 2016
February 25: *In Sinu Jesu*, February 25, 2016
February 26: *In Sinu Jesu*, February 13, 2009
February 27: *In Sinu Jesu*, February 8, 2010
February 28: *In Sinu Jesu*, February 6, 2008
February 29: *In Sinu Jesu*, January 31, 2008

MARCH

March 1: *In Sinu Jesu*, March 1, 2010
March 2: *In Sinu Jesu*, November 6, 2011
March 3: *In Sinu Jesu*, March 3, 2010
March 4: *In Sinu Jesu*, March 3, 2016
March 5: *In Sinu Jesu*, March 5, 2010
March 6: *In Sinu Jesu*, March 6, 2012
March 7: *In Sinu Jesu*, March 7, 2008
March 8: *In Sinu Jesu*, March 8, 2010
March 9: *In Sinu Jesu*, March 8, 2010
March 10: *In Sinu Jesu*, March 10, 2012
March 11: *In Sinu Jesu*, March 1, 2010
March 12: *In Sinu Jesu*, March 13, 2010
March 13: *In Sinu Jesu*, March 13, 2010

March 14: *In Sinu Jesu*, March 14, 2009
March 15: *In Sinu Jesu*, March 15, 2009
March 16: *In Sinu Jesu*, March 16, 2009
March 17: *In Sinu Jesu*, March 15, 2010
March 18: *In Sinu Jesu*, March 13, 2012
March 19: *In Sinu Jesu*, March 13, 2009
March 20: *In Sinu Jesu*, March 20, 2008
March 21: *In Sinu Jesu*, March 21, 2009
March 22: *In Sinu Jesu*, March 22, 2010
March 23: *In Sinu Jesu*, March 23, 2009
March 24: *In Sinu Jesu*, March 24, 2016
March 25: *In Sinu Jesu*, March 25, 2009
March 26: *In Sinu Jesu*, March 3, 2016
March 27: *In Sinu Jesu*, March 27, 2008
March 28: *In Sinu Jesu*, March 28, 2008
March 29: *In Sinu Jesu*, March 29, 2008
March 30: *In Sinu Jesu*, March 30, 2008
March 31: *In Sinu Jesu*, March 31, 2016

APRIL

April 1: *In Sinu Jesu*, March 22, 2010
April 2: *In Sinu Jesu*, March 16, 2010
April 3: *In Sinu Jesu*, April 3, 2008
April 4: *In Sinu Jesu*, March 16, 2010
April 5: *In Sinu Jesu*, March 30, 2008
April 6: *In Sinu Jesu*, March 8, 2010
April 7: *In Sinu Jesu*, April 7, 2016
April 8: *In Sinu Jesu*, April 7, 2016
April 9: *In Sinu Jesu*, January 31, 2008

April 10: *In Sinu Jesu*, April 10, 2008
April 11: *In Sinu Jesu*, April 11, 2010
April 12: *In Sinu Jesu*, April 11, 2010
April 13: *In Sinu Jesu*, April 15, 2010
April 14: *In Sinu Jesu*, September 25, 2011
April 15: *In Sinu Jesu*, April 15, 2010
April 16: *In Sinu Jesu*, April 15, 2010
April 17: *In Sinu Jesu*, April 17, 2008
April 18: *In Sinu Jesu*, April 14, 2010
April 19: *In Sinu Jesu*, April 7, 2016
April 20: *In Sinu Jesu*, April 20, 2012
April 21: *In Sinu Jesu*, April 24, 2008
April 22: *In Sinu Jesu*, April 24, 2008
April 23: *In Sinu Jesu*, April 23, 2012
April 24: *In Sinu Jesu*, April 24, 2008
April 25: *In Sinu Jesu*, April 24, 2008
April 26: *In Sinu Jesu*, April 11, 2010
April 27: *In Sinu Jesu*, April 11, 2010
April 28: *In Sinu Jesu*, March 2, 2010
April 29: *In Sinu Jesu*, April 29, 2011
April 30: *In Sinu Jesu*, April 24, 2008

MAY

May 1: *In Sinu Jesu*, May 1, 2008
May 2: *In Sinu Jesu*, May 2, 2010
May 3: *In Sinu Jesu*, December 3, 2014
May 4: *In Sinu Jesu*, May 7, 2010
May 5: *In Sinu Jesu*, May 7, 2010
May 6: *In Sinu Jesu*, May 8, 2008

May 7: *In Sinu Jesu*, May 7, 2010
May 8: *In Sinu Jesu*, May 8, 2008
May 9: *In Sinu Jesu*, March 1, 2010
May 10: *In Sinu Jesu*, May 12, 2009
May 11: *In Sinu Jesu*, May 12, 2009
May 12: *In Sinu Jesu*, May 12, 2009
May 13: *In Sinu Jesu*, May 16, 2010
May 14: *In Sinu Jesu*, May 17, 2012
May 15: *In Sinu Jesu*, May 15, 2008
May 16: *In Sinu Jesu*, May 16, 2010
May 17: *In Sinu Jesu*, May 17, 2012
May 18: *In Sinu Jesu*, May 22, 2008
May 19: *In Sinu Jesu*, May 29, 2010
May 20: *In Sinu Jesu*, January 26, 2010
May 21: *In Sinu Jesu*, March 13, 2010
May 22: *In Sinu Jesu*, May 22, 2008
May 23: *In Sinu Jesu*, March 2, 2010
May 24: *In Sinu Jesu*, May 7, 2010
May 25: *In Sinu Jesu*, May 25, 2010
May 26: *In Sinu Jesu*, May 29, 2014
May 27: *In Sinu Jesu*, May 27, 2012
May 28: *In Sinu Jesu*, May 28, 2010
May 29: *In Sinu Jesu*, May 29, 2010
May 30: *In Sinu Jesu*, May 29, 2008
May 31: *In Sinu Jesu*, May 29, 2014

JUNE
June 1: *In Sinu Jesu*, June 2, 2012
June 2: *In Sinu Jesu*, June 2, 2012

June 3: *In Sinu Jesu*, June 9, 2012
June 4: *In Sinu Jesu*, June 9, 2012
June 5: *In Sinu Jesu*, June 9, 2012
June 6: *In Sinu Jesu*, June 11, 2008
June 7: *In Sinu Jesu*, June 9, 2012
June 8: *In Sinu Jesu*, June 12, 2008
June 9: *In Sinu Jesu*, June 9, 2012
June 10: *In Sinu Jesu*, June 15, 2013
June 11: *In Sinu Jesu*, June 11, 2008
June 12: *In Sinu Jesu*, June 12, 2008
June 13: *In Sinu Jesu*, June 15, 2013
June 14: *In Sinu Jesu*, June 15, 2013
June 15: *In Sinu Jesu*, June 15, 2013
June 16: *In Sinu Jesu*, June 17, 2008
June 17: *In Sinu Jesu*, June 17, 2008
June 18: *In Sinu Jesu*, June 18, 2009
June 19: *In Sinu Jesu*, June 19, 2008
June 20: *In Sinu Jesu*, June 22, 2012
June 21: *In Sinu Jesu*, June 23, 2009
June 22: *In Sinu Jesu*, June 22, 2009
June 23: *In Sinu Jesu*, June 23, 2009
June 24: *In Sinu Jesu*, June 19, 2008
June 25: *In Sinu Jesu*, June 18, 2009
June 26: *In Sinu Jesu*, June 26, 2008
June 27: *In Sinu Jesu*, December 6, 2014
June 28: *In Sinu Jesu*, June 19, 2008
June 29: *In Sinu Jesu*, June 18, 2009
June 30: *In Sinu Jesu*, June 23, 2009

JULY

July 1: *In Sinu Jesu*, September 7, 2011
July 2: *In Sinu Jesu*, September 5, 2011
July 3: *In Sinu Jesu*, July 3, 2008
July 4: *In Sinu Jesu*, April 15, 2010
July 5: *In Sinu Jesu*, September 5, 2011
July 6: *In Sinu Jesu*, July 6, 2012
July 7: *In Sinu Jesu*, July 7, 2009
July 8: *In Sinu Jesu*, July 10, 2008
July 9: *In Sinu Jesu*, July 9, 2009
July 10: *In Sinu Jesu*, July 10, 2009
July 11: *In Sinu Jesu*, July 11, 2009
July 12: *In Sinu Jesu*, July 12, 2009
July 13: *In Sinu Jesu*, July 26, 2012
July 14: *In Sinu Jesu*, July 17, 2008
July 15: *In Sinu Jesu*, July 15, 2012
July 16: *In Sinu Jesu*, July 24, 2008
July 17: *In Sinu Jesu*, July 17, 2008
July 18: *In Sinu Jesu*, July 3, 2008
July 19: *In Sinu Jesu*, June 23, 2009
July 20: *In Sinu Jesu*, January 27, 2012
July 21: *In Sinu Jesu*, July 26, 2012
July 22: *In Sinu Jesu*, March 2, 2010
July 23: *In Sinu Jesu*, June 18, 2009
July 24: *In Sinu Jesu*, July 24, 2008
July 25: *In Sinu Jesu*, July 15, 2012
July 26: *In Sinu Jesu*, July 26, 2012
July 27: *In Sinu Jesu*, July 9, 2009
July 28: *In Sinu Jesu*, July 12, 2009

July 29: *In Sinu Jesu*, July 24, 2008
July 30: *In Sinu Jesu*, July 11, 2011
July 31: *In Sinu Jesu*, July 31, 2008

AUGUST

August 1: *In Sinu Jesu*, August 7, 2008
August 2: *In Sinu Jesu*, August 26, 2010
August 3: *In Sinu Jesu*, August 26, 2010
August 4: *In Sinu Jesu*, August 26, 2010
August 5: *In Sinu Jesu*, August 22, 2011
August 6: *In Sinu Jesu*, August 25, 2008
August 7: *In Sinu Jesu*, August 7, 2008
August 8: *In Sinu Jesu*, August 27, 2011
August 9: *In Sinu Jesu*, August 9, 2011
August 10: *In Sinu Jesu*, July 31, 2008
August 11: *In Sinu Jesu*, August 25, 2008
August 12: *In Sinu Jesu*, August 7, 2011
August 13: *In Sinu Jesu*, August 7, 2008
August 14: *In Sinu Jesu*, August 7, 2008
August 15: *In Sinu Jesu*, August 7, 2008
August 16: *In Sinu Jesu*, August 7, 2008
August 17: *In Sinu Jesu*, August 22, 2011
August 18: *In Sinu Jesu*, September 7, 2011
August 19: *In Sinu Jesu*, September 1, 2011
August 20: *In Sinu Jesu*, January 27, 2012
August 21: *In Sinu Jesu*, August 27, 2011
August 22: *In Sinu Jesu*, August 22, 2011
August 23: *In Sinu Jesu*, August 23, 2011
August 24: *In Sinu Jesu*, August 24, 2008

August 25: *In Sinu Jesu*, August 25, 2008
August 26: *In Sinu Jesu*, August 26, 2010
August 27: *In Sinu Jesu*, April 15, 2010
August 28: *In Sinu Jesu*, April 15, 2010
August 29: *In Sinu Jesu*, April 15, 2010
August 30: *In Sinu Jesu*, April 15, 2010
August 31: *In Sinu Jesu*, April 15, 2010

SEPTEMBER

September 1: *In Sinu Jesu*, September 1, 2011
September 2: *In Sinu Jesu*, September 5, 2011
September 3: *In Sinu Jesu*, August 26, 2010
September 4: *In Sinu Jesu*, September 7, 2011
September 5: *In Sinu Jesu*, September 5, 2011
September 6: *In Sinu Jesu*, September 6, 2011
September 7: *In Sinu Jesu*, September 7, 2011
September 8: *In Sinu Jesu*, September 7, 2013
September 9: *In Sinu Jesu*, July 31, 2008
September 10: *In Sinu Jesu*, September 5, 2011
September 11: *In Sinu Jesu*, September 7, 2013
September 12: *In Sinu Jesu*, September 1, 2011
September 13: *In Sinu Jesu*, September 7, 2011
September 14: *In Sinu Jesu*, September 7, 2011
September 15: *In Sinu Jesu*, September 15, 2011
September 16: *In Sinu Jesu*, September 16, 2011
September 17: *In Sinu Jesu*, September 25, 2011
September 18: *In Sinu Jesu*, September 25, 2011
September 19: *In Sinu Jesu*, Vigil of October 13, 2007
September 20: *In Sinu Jesu*, September 20, 2011

September 21: *In Sinu Jesu*, Vigil of October 13, 2007
September 22: *In Sinu Jesu*, September 22, 2011
September 23: *In Sinu Jesu*, September 23, 2011
September 24: *In Sinu Jesu*, January 27, 2012
September 25: *In Sinu Jesu*, September 25, 2011
September 26: *In Sinu Jesu*, September 26, 2011
September 27: *In Sinu Jesu*, October 17, 2011
September 28: *In Sinu Jesu*, September 28, 2011
September 29: *In Sinu Jesu*, October 17, 2008
September 30: *In Sinu Jesu*, October 17, 2008

OCTOBER

October 1: *In Sinu Jesu*, October 1, 2011
October 2: *In Sinu Jesu*, December 2, 2014
October 3: *In Sinu Jesu*, October 9, 2011
October 4: *In Sinu Jesu*, October 10, 2007
October 5: *In Sinu Jesu*, October 5, 2007
October 6: *In Sinu Jesu*, October 6, 2011
October 7: *In Sinu Jesu*, December 11, 2007
October 8: *In Sinu Jesu*, October 8, 2007
October 9: *In Sinu Jesu*, October 9, 2011
October 10: *In Sinu Jesu*, October 10, 2007
October 11: *In Sinu Jesu*, October 19, 2008
October 12: *In Sinu Jesu*, October 25, 2008
October 13: *In Sinu Jesu*, Vigil of October 13, 2007
October 14: *In Sinu Jesu*, October 25, 2008
October 15: *In Sinu Jesu*, October 15, 2011
October 16: *In Sinu Jesu*, October 25, 2008
October 17: *In Sinu Jesu*, October 17, 2011

October 18: *In Sinu Jesu*, October 19, 2008
October 19: *In Sinu Jesu*, October 19, 2008
October 20: *In Sinu Jesu*, October 25, 2008
October 21: *In Sinu Jesu*, December 2, 2014
October 22: *In Sinu Jesu*, October 29, 2011
October 23: *In Sinu Jesu*, October 29, 2007
October 24: *In Sinu Jesu*, October 29, 2011
October 25: *In Sinu Jesu*, October 25, 2008
October 26: *In Sinu Jesu*, September 23, 2011
October 27: *In Sinu Jesu*, November 12, 2011
October 28: *In Sinu Jesu*, October 28, 2007
October 29: *In Sinu Jesu*, October 29, 2007
October 30: *In Sinu Jesu*, October 29, 2007
October 31: *In Sinu Jesu*, October 29, 2007

NOVEMBER

November 1: *In Sinu Jesu*, November 10, 2008
November 2: *In Sinu Jesu*, November 10, 2008
November 3: *In Sinu Jesu*, November 3, 2011
November 4: *In Sinu Jesu*, November 6, 2011
November 5: *In Sinu Jesu*, November 6, 2011
November 6: *In Sinu Jesu*, November 6, 2011
November 7: *In Sinu Jesu*, November 29, 2008
November 8: *In Sinu Jesu*, November 12, 2011
November 9: *In Sinu Jesu*, November 10, 2008
November 10: *In Sinu Jesu*, November 10, 2008
November 11: *In Sinu Jesu*, November 12, 2008
November 12: *In Sinu Jesu*, November 12, 2008
November 13: *In Sinu Jesu*, November 13, 2008

November 14: *In Sinu Jesu*, November 16, 2011
November 15: *In Sinu Jesu*, November 15, 2013
November 16: *In Sinu Jesu*, November 16, 2011
November 17: *In Sinu Jesu*, November 29, 2008
November 18: *In Sinu Jesu*, November 28, 2014
November 19: *In Sinu Jesu*, November 19, 2011
November 20: *In Sinu Jesu*, November 28, 2014
November 21: *In Sinu Jesu*, November 21, 2011
November 22: *In Sinu Jesu*, November 28, 2014
November 23: *In Sinu Jesu*, November 12, 2011
November 24: *In Sinu Jesu*, November 28, 2014
November 25: *In Sinu Jesu*, November 21, 2011
November 26: *In Sinu Jesu*, November 3, 2011
November 27: *In Sinu Jesu*, November 15, 2013
November 28: *In Sinu Jesu*, November 28, 2014
November 29: *In Sinu Jesu*, November 29, 2008
November 30: *In Sinu Jesu*, November 28, 2014

DECEMBER

December 1: *In Sinu Jesu*, November 6, 2011
December 2: *In Sinu Jesu*, December 2, 2014
December 3: *In Sinu Jesu*, December 3, 2014
December 4: *In Sinu Jesu*, October 28, 2007
December 5: *In Sinu Jesu*, November 19, 2011
December 6: *In Sinu Jesu*, December 6, 2014
December 7: *In Sinu Jesu*, December 3, 2009
December 8: *In Sinu Jesu*, December 9, 2007
December 9: *In Sinu Jesu*, December 8, 2007
December 10: *In Sinu Jesu*, December 10, 2007

December 11: *In Sinu Jesu*, December 11, 2007
December 12: *In Sinu Jesu*, October 10, 2007
December 13: *In Sinu Jesu*, December 13, 2009
December 14: *In Sinu Jesu*, September 20, 2011
December 15: *In Sinu Jesu*, December 27, 2011
December 16: *In Sinu Jesu*, October 25, 2008
December 17: *In Sinu Jesu*, October 6, 2011
December 18: *In Sinu Jesu*, December 6, 2014
December 19: *In Sinu Jesu*, December 19, 2007
December 20: *In Sinu Jesu*, December 20, 2011
December 21: *In Sinu Jesu*, December 27, 2011
December 22: *In Sinu Jesu*, September 23, 2011
December 23: *In Sinu Jesu*, October 6, 2011
December 24: *In Sinu Jesu*, December 19, 2007
December 25: *In Sinu Jesu*, December 27, 2011
December 26: *In Sinu Jesu*, September 22, 2011
December 27: *In Sinu Jesu*, December 27, 2011
December 28: *In Sinu Jesu*, July 3, 2008
December 29: *In Sinu Jesu*, December 27, 2011
December 30: *In Sinu Jesu*, January 7, 2012
December 31: *In Sinu Jesu*, January 10, 2012

www.ingramcontent.com/pod-product-compliance
Lightning Source LLC
Chambersburg PA
CBHW020347170426
43200CB00005B/72